We Believe:
Forty Meditations on the
Nicene Creed

cy May !
Yor And Y
With His great
Love And
Peace !
Richard
Maffeo

By Richard Maffeo

xulon PRESS

For Mom.
Thank you for all you've done.

For my wife, Nancy.
You are my inspiration

A special thanks to Gail Welborn, for exquisitely helpful critique of this work.

Author photograph by Yufeng Miller of E-photography

Richard Maffeo, a convert to Catholicism from evangelical Protestant faith, wrote these meditations based on the Nicene Creed to stir a passion within the hearts of his fellow Catholics – a passion "for the faith that was once for all handed down to the holy ones." (Jude 1:3)

Whether you've confessed the Nicene Creed for as long as you can remember, or rarely recited the words spoken by Saints and sinners for nearly seventeen hundred years, these forty meditations offer a fresh perspective on our ancient proclamation of Christian faith.

Let these meditations guide your contemplation of the Mystery of the Triune God. Explore the wonder of God's love, His faithfulness and compassion toward you. You might never say the Nicene Creed the same way again.

The Nicene Creed*

We believe in one God,
the Father, the Almighty,
maker of heaven and earth,
of all that is seen and unseen.
We believe in one Lord, Jesus Christ,
the only Son of God,
eternally begotten of the Father,
God from God, Light from Light,
true God from true God,
begotten, not made,
one in Being with the Father.
Through Him all things were made.
For us men and for our salvation
He came down from heaven.
By the power of the Holy Spirit
He was born of the Virgin Mary, and became man.
For our sake He was crucified under Pontius Pilate;
He suffered, died, and was buried.
On the third day He rose again
in fulfillment of the Scriptures;
He ascended into heaven,

and is seated at the right hand of the Father.
He will come again in glory to judge the living
and the dead,
and His kingdom will have no end.
We believe in the Holy Spirit, the Lord, the giver of Life,
who proceeds from the Father and the Son.
With the Father and the Son, He is worshiped and glorified.
He has spoken through the Prophets.
We believe in one holy catholic and apostolic Church.
We acknowledge one baptism for the forgiveness of sins.
We look for the resurrection of the dead,
and the life of the world to come. Amen.

*The Nicene Creed, originally written in Greek, has been translated into many languages. The English translation in this book is from the current edition of the Roman Missal used in the United States.

Introduction

I drive twenty miles to work each morning. I do the same twenty back home in the evening. Two hundred miles a week. Eight hundred a month. When I first took the job, I put the Chevy on cruise control; but after two weeks turned it off. The drive is monotonous enough without removing the excitement of holding a steady foot on the accelerator. The commute is so mind numbing, I've sometimes pulled into the parking lot not remembering the drive – and that's a little disturbing. Monotony can lead to complacency, complacency to carelessness. For some activities, carelessness can be dangerous. Like driving.

Or worship.

Many years ago, my wife and I regularly attended a local synagogue for Sabbath services. Although we were Christians, I enjoyed the Jewish liturgy and rhythm of the rituals because they reminded me of my Jewish upbringing. During each Sabbath service, Jews sing the Sh'ma – an ancient declaration of Jewish faith taken directly from Deuteronomy chapter six: *Sh'ma Yisrael, Adonai Elohenu, Adonai echod* – Hear, oh Israel, the Lord our God, the Lord is one. The Sh'ma is so important in Jewish religious history that persecuted Jews have died with those words on their lips in a final testament to their faith.

One Sabbath as we sang the text I noticed a middle-aged man a few pews to my left singing with the rest of us, but his attention was focused on his fingernails. I watched in dumbfounded disbelief as he cleaned his nails with a toothpick – yet all the while singing Israel's most profound declaration of faith.

Like the Sh'ma, the Nicene Creed is a profound statement of Christian faith, rich with history and application even for the 21st century Church. Those ancient words remain central to the mystical depth of Christianity. They capture the essence of our belief in the Holy Trinity, the incarnation of Christ, His atonement, and resurrection. It proclaims forgiveness of sins, the role of the Church in our salvation and the imminent return of our Savior. Surely, without those essential tenets, the foundation of our faith rests on sand.

The doctrine of the Trinity begins unfolding with the words, "We believe in one God." Christians understand the nuance – one God, yet three Persons. The unveiling continues as we proclaim the Father Almighty. We move to the second Person of the Godhead, Jesus Christ, "God from God, Light from Light, true God from true God." We focus next on the third Person, the Holy Spirit who, "with the Father and the Son" is worshiped and glorified.

The majestic truths continue; God from God became flesh and blood in the incarnation through the Virgin Mary. The atonement assures humanity that Christ's blood can cleanse the deepest sin. The Resurrection, Christ's ascension to the Father, and the creation of the Church, all demonstrate the depth and breadth of the ineffable grandeur of God's love and purpose to reconcile humankind with Himself.

But like some who sing the Sh'ma, it is possible for majestic truth to become rote, for us to mouth words while – figuratively, if not actually – cleaning our fingernails.

When we gather and testify to our faith, we do so in union – and Communion – with two thousand years of prophets and apostles, priests and laity, saints and sinners, all who proclaimed – as we proclaim – "We believe."

These forty meditations will provide good opportunity to turn off our spiritual cruise control. The highway is rife with potholes, and if we're not careful, we could find ourselves broken down on the side of the road. But if we pay attention to what we say at each Mass, we might be surprised by what we hear.

Creed Statement: We believe in one God, the Father, the Almighty, maker of heaven and earth, of all that is seen and unseen.

Today's Focus: **WE** believe

Now the body is not a single part, but many. If a foot should say, "Because I am not a hand I do not belong to the body," it does not for this reason belong any less to the body... But God has so constructed the body as to give greater honor to a part that is without it, so that there may be no division in the body, but that the parts may have the same concern for one another... Now you are Christ's body, and individually parts of it (1 Corinthians 12:14-27).

In December 1917, Father Edward Flanagan established a community near Omaha, Nebraska for homeless boys. The well-known sculpture of an older boy carrying a younger one on his back symbolizes Flanagan's community. The story behind the monument is rooted in a sweltering summer day when a group from the orphanage headed to a nearby water hole to swim. One of boys couldn't go because his leg was in a brace. When another youngster, Jim, lifted him onto his back, Father Flanagan asked the others to help, but Jim waved him off.

"He ain't heavy, Father," Jim said. "He's my brother."

When the Church says *we*, she affirms God is *our* Father, those who love Christ are our spiritual brothers and sisters, and – and this is important – that we are *responsible* for each other. John Donne, a 17th century Churchman and poet, understood what some today seem to have forgotten. "The church is Catholic, universal," he wrote. "When she baptizes a child, that action concerns me, for that child is thereby... ingrafted into that body whereof I am a member... No man is an island, entire of itself; every man is a piece of the continent, a part of the main."

That is why, though some later versions of the Nicene Creed replace *we* with *I*, I prefer the first person plural because it reminds me of my "part of the main." *We* lifts me to see beyond myself and acknowledge my responsibility to the community of other believers.

The next time you recite the Creed during Mass, look at your Christian brothers and sisters in the pews near you. They are your *family*, and you have the great privilege to help them carry their burdens and, as St. Paul wrote, "fulfill the law of Christ" (Galatians 6:2).

Prayer (of St. Francis): *Lord, make me an instrument of Your peace. Where there is hatred, let me sow love; where there is injury, pardon; where there is doubt, faith; where there is despair, hope; where there is darkness, light; and where there is sadness, joy. Oh, Divine Master, grant that I may not so much seek to be consoled as to console; to be understood as to understand; to be loved as to love; for it is in giving that we receive; it is in pardoning that we are pardoned; and it is in dying that we are born to eternal life. Amen.*

Creed Statement: We believe in one God, the Father, the Almighty, maker of heaven and earth, of all that is seen and unseen.

Today's Focus: We **BELIEVE**

Trust in the LORD with all your heart, on your own intelligence rely not; In all your ways be mindful of Him, and He will make straight your paths
(Proverbs 3:5-6).

I had heard about the rappelling tower. Its reputation loomed larger than life weeks before my arrival in San Antonio for military training. I stood in line with two dozen others and stared soberly at the fifty-three-foot rickety wooden structure. My palms start to sweat when I stand on a chair.

"Pick up the rope in front of you." The sergeant's bark broke into my thoughts.

With a series of twists and jerks, he led us in wrapping the rope around, under, and behind our waist and thighs to form a saddle. Then he marched us to the ladder and we climbed toward the clouds. Clumps of dirt fell from the boots of those ahead of me.

When the last straggler took her place on the platform, the sergeant asked, "Who's afraid of heights?"

I raised my hand, fervently hoping he'd send me back down the ladder. I was wrong.

"You're first," he said.

With the proverbial patience of Job, the sergeant fastened a rope through the "D" ring and guided it around to my back. My stomach churned as I stepped toward the ledge. Like a robot, I obeyed the sergeant's instructions and grabbed the line in front of me with my left hand and the line behind me with my right. The tail end fell what seemed five miles to the ground.

Sweat dripped from my forehead as I leaned back into space. Resigned to my fate, I let out a few inches of rope. In a moment, I was perpendicular to the tower wall, fifty-three very long feet above the Texas soil.

"Jump!" the sergeant commanded.

I pushed away from the wall and plummeted toward earth until I gripped the rope and stopped my descent. Euphoria swelled in my chest when I realized I was still alive. I pushed again and fell another twenty feet. One more shove and I landed gently on Texas soil.

Sometimes my struggle with confidence in God's power, presence, and love is a little like my struggle with that monstrous fifty-three-foot tower. Biblical faith is more than intellectual assent to God's existence. It is God-centered and births an active, risk-taking confidence that proclaims, "I will trust God no matter where He leads and no matter what He tells me to do."

Just as I needed to believe the rope would hold me, I need to believe God will not leave me hanging in space – or let me fall. And though I might wonder if the Father really knows how far it is to the bottom, I've also experienced what the Psalmist learned, "Those whose steps are guided by the Lord, whose way God approves, may stumble, but they will never fall, for the Lord holds their hand" (Psalm 37:23-24).

That's one of the things the Creed helps us remember – not only *what* we believe, but in *whom* we believe. No wonder you and I can trust Him, even if He asks us to lean into His arms and dangle fifty-three feet above the ground.

Prayer: *Lord, I believe in You. Increase my faith. I trust in You. Strengthen my trust. I love You. Let me love You more and more.* (Pope Clement XI)

Creed Statement: We believe in one God, the Father, the Almighty, maker of heaven and earth, of all that is seen and unseen.

Today's Focus: **One God**

For though the fig tree blossom not, nor fruit be on the vines, though the yield of the olive fail and the terraces produce no nourishment, though the flocks disappear from the fold and there be no herd in the stalls, yet will I rejoice in the Lord and exult in my saving God (Habakkuk 3:17-18).

Throughout history, many cultures have embraced polytheism. I wonder if one reason they did so was an attempt to explain the sudden disasters humankind experiences. Perhaps they reasoned that if one god controlled human affairs, random tragedies wouldn't occur. Earthquakes, tornados, and floods were likely the result of gods competing for dominance over our world.

Christians reject polytheism for many good reasons. Let's look at two.

First, we recognize our limitation to discover answers to life's unpredictable troubles. How can the finite comprehend the infinite, the created the Creator, the pot the potter? This was the problem Job and his counselors bandied for the first 37 chapters of that Old Testament book. They never came up with a satisfactory answer, and when God broke into their debate, He moved beyond their arguments to a more fundamental issue: Who were *they* to question God? (Chapters 38-42).

Second, we know God reveals His existence in various ways. His magnificence permeates nature. The psalmist wrote, "The heavens declare the glory of God; the sky proclaims its builder's craft" (Psalm 19:2-5). He declared through the prophets, "I am the first and I am the last; there is no God but Me" (Isaiah 44:6). And He revealed His mercy through His Son, "In these last days, (God) spoke to us through a Son, whom He made heir of all things and through whom He created the universe, who is the radiance of his glory, the very imprint of his being, and who sustains all things by his mighty word" (Hebrews 1:1-3).

The very first sentence of the Creed captures the essence of a foundational truth: God is one. Inherent in that statement is also our declaration that despite life's unexpected hardships and tragedies, we will never turn from serving Him. If mountains fall into the sea, if the earth shakes loose everything we thought secure, God is still God.

And we will bow to no other.

Prayer: *Who is like You, Oh Lord, my God? Who can compare with Your power, majesty or mercy? You are my Creator. I belong to You. I give You my heart and my life. I will honor no other gods, no idols, no masters before You. Amen.*

Creed Statement: We believe in one God, the Father, the Almighty, maker of heaven and earth, of all that is seen and unseen.

Today's Focus: **The Father**

[Jesus] came to what was His own, but His own people did not accept Him. But to those who did accept Him He gave power to become children of God, to those who believe in His name, who were born not by natural generation nor by human choice nor by a man's decision but of God (John 1:11-13).

Fifty years. That's how long it's been since my father abandoned me. The day is tattooed into my memory. I remember where I sat and what I was doing when Mom told me Daddy would never be coming home.

My father was never there when I had problems with school, or friends, or when I started dating. He never attended my school plays or high school football games. He never showed up at my Boy Scout award ceremonies, never saw me graduate high school or college, get married, and raise children. When I searched for him years later, he wrote back a scathing reply and ordered me to leave him alone.

As my five-year-old mind tried to absorb Mom's words that somber day in 1955, I didn't know my heavenly Father was there, sitting on the couch with me. I didn't know He embraced me as I walked to Dad's closet, took his favorite tie, and hid it, hoping to force him to stay with us. I didn't know God stood beside me during my teen years when I got snared in a revolving door of drugs, sexual immoralities, fights and thefts. I didn't know He wept with me as I sobbed on my sister's shoulder, "I never had a father. I never had a father."

"We believe in one God, the Father, the Almighty."

There are times no other words speak more powerfully to my emotions – God, the Father. Sometimes I sense Him so near I can feel His warmth. When I meet Him in prayer, I can feel Him draw me into His arms. If I listen carefully, I hear Him whisper, "I will never leave you. I will never forsake you."

What do you think about when you think about God as your Father? Perhaps your relationship mirrors mine. Maybe it was better, or much worse. Whatever our memory, of one thing we can be certain: Calvary proves for all time and into eternity, "Even if my father and mother forsake me, the Lord will take me in"(Psalm 27:10). Through Isaiah God promised, "Can a mother forget her infant, be without tenderness for the child of her womb? Even should she forget, I will never forget you. See, upon the palms of My hands I have written your name; your walls are ever before Me" (Isaiah 49:15-16).

As we recite those simple words of the Creed – The Father – we remind ourselves the God of the *universe* is our Father.

Why do we sometimes doubt that?

Prayer: (From Psalm 103): *Lord, You are compassionate and abounding in love. As high as the heavens are above the earth, so great is Your love for those who fear You. For the sake of Christ's sacrifice, You remove our transgressions from us as far as east is from west. As a father has compassion on his children, so You have compassion on those who call to You for mercy. Have mercy on us, Father. We are Your people, born by faith in the atoning blood of Your Son, Jesus. Amen.*

Creed Statement: We believe in one God, the Father, the Almighty, maker of heaven and earth, of all that is seen and unseen.

Today's focus: **Almighty**

A throne was there in heaven, and on the throne sat one whose appearance sparkled like jasper and carnelian... From the throne came flashes of lightning, rumblings, and peals of thunder. Seven flaming torches burned in front of the throne... (and) four living creatures... do not stop exclaiming: "Holy, holy, holy is the Lord God almighty, who was, and who is, and who is to come (Revelation 4:2-8).

For seven fear-filled years, the Midianites spread terror across Israel. Bands of marauders ravaged villages, slaughtered men, women, and children and stole their possessions. Israelites lived like hunted animals, hiding in caves and along cliffs. Gideon was one of those Israelites. Then one day, as he threshed his meager wheat harvest, an angel called to him, "The Lord is with you, O champion" (Judges 6:12).

But Gideon answered, "If the Lord is with us, why has all this happened to us?" A moment later he added, "And where are the miracles we've heard about all our lives?"

It's easy for me to point a finger at Gideon and scoff that anyone could think the days of God's miracles were over. Yet, I can't tell you how many times I've thought, "God answered my prayers in the past, but how can I be sure He will do it again? God took care of us before, but will He do it now?"

Like Gideon, I believe in the almighty God of the past, but I'm not convinced He's the same God of the now – or the future.

What nonsense. If you remember the text in Judges, Gideon – and three hundred men armed with nothing more than clay pots, torches, and their faith – won a miraculous victory for Israel.

What do we call our Midianites? Is it illness? Unemployment? Divorce? If faith teaches us anything, it's this: God is never limited by time or resources. What He opens, none can close. What He shuts none can open. God is our Almighty *Father*. Compassionate. Involved. He knows the number of hairs on our heads, the thoughts in our hearts, and our words before they cross our lips. A sparrow won't fall to the ground without His knowledge – and you and I are of much greater value to God than a sparrow (Matthew 10:29-31).

It's easy to recite Creeds and believe in past answers to prayer. But when the doctor's report takes our breath away, when floods engulf our homes, when fires consume our livelihood – the words of the Creed, "We believe in the Father Almighty," can be an immovable rock and a shout of victory for those who trust Him – even to the jaws of death.

Gideon believed the days of God's mighty works were over. Let's not make the same error. Our God and Father is the same yesterday, today and forever.

Prayer: *Lord, I need You. Be my shield and companion, my strength and tireless resource. Be my comfort and guide. I lose focus when life's storms shake my faith, when windstorms uproot my confidence in Your might and mercy. Send Your Holy Spirit into my heart and nurture my trust in Your everlasting power and love. Amen.*

Creed Statement: We believe in one God, the Father, the Almighty, maker of heaven and earth, of all that is seen and unseen.

Today's Focus: **Maker of heaven and earth**

Then I saw a new heaven and a new earth. The former heaven and the former earth had passed away, and the sea was no more... I heard a loud voice from the throne saying, "Behold, God's dwelling is with the human race... He will wipe every tear from their eyes, and there shall be no more death or mourning, wailing or pain (Revelation 21:1-4).

When our children were younger, my wife and I could predict their question as surely as the sunrise. Whether we drove to the zoo on the other side of town or to friends in another city, every few minutes – or so it seemed – they asked, "Are we there yet?"

And each time, I assured them, "Soon. Very soon, and we'll be there."

I understood their excitement – or was it impatience? Their young lives rambled along with carefree simplicity, snug within the safety and love of our home. Life doesn't get any better. A broken dolly? No problem. Daddy will fix it.

Skinned your knee? Let me kiss and make it better. Hungry? Daddy will make you a snack.

When I took time to see life through their eyes, I caught snatches of a passion I left behind in my own childhood, an effervescence muted by maturity – not that there is anything wrong with maturity, except when it reduces childlike eagerness to a bored yawn.

But sometimes, while I meditate on these words of the Creed, a renewed excitement strains for freedom. Perhaps it's because as an adult I realize life *can* get better than this. It *will* get better. The older I grow, the better I know I cannot fix every broken dolly or heal every hurt knee. And I catch myself asking Father with increasing frequency, every few minutes - or so it seems, "Are we there, yet? When will we be home?"

Our Almighty *Father* is maker of heaven and earth. I don't know much about heaven, but I know plenty about the home we call earth. Natural disasters and human-created catastrophes send our planet reeling under a magma flow of death, destruction, and anguish. Whose heart doesn't long for that Day when Father will fix it, and heal it? Who doesn't long for that Day when God wipes away our tears and puts an end to death and mourning?

Are we there yet, Lord? How much longer until we're home?

And sometimes, if I listen carefully enough, I can hear Him whisper, "Soon. Very soon, and we'll be there."

Prayer: *Come quickly, Lord Jesus. And while we await Your new heaven and earth, create in us clean hearts and renewed spirits. Help us promote justice, mercy and peace in our world. Awaken us to the holy. Through us reconcile enemies, impassion our parishes and heal the divisions in Your Church. Amen.*

Creed Statement: We believe in one God, the Father, the Almighty, maker of heaven and earth, of all that is seen and unseen.

Today's Focus: **All that is seen and unseen**

Bartimaeus, a blind man, the son of Timaeus, sat by the roadside begging. On hearing that it was Jesus of Nazareth, he began to cry out and say, "Jesus, son of David, have pity on me."… Jesus said to him in reply, "What do you want me to do for you?" The blind man replied to Him, "Master, I want to see" (Mark 46-51).

Yogi Berra, former catcher for the NY Yankees and manager of the Mets, Yankees and Houston Astros, is well known for pithy quips like, "If you come to a fork in the road, take it," and, "It's like déjà vu all over again." My favorite is, "You can see a lot just by looking."

During my teen years, I repeatedly closed my eyes to things I didn't want to see. I remember one evening in particular. As I walked toward my apartment, I noticed an anthill outside my door. Hundreds of ants scurried in and around their mound and a lesson I'd learned in high school biology came to mind. Without tiny creatures like ants, topsoil irrigation couldn't occur. Plant life, as we know it, couldn't exist.

In that moment of reflection, I realized a precise order of life existed all around me. But order requires someone to do the ordering, and I immediately realized where that thought would take me. So I closed my spiritual eyes because I didn't want to go there. I had eyes only for young women, drugs, and parties. I knew God and my lusts couldn't peacefully coexist, so I ignored the anthill. I preferred to keep God in the psychological cubbyhole I'd labeled, "Not Sure Of," where He joined other problematic nuisances like "Absolute Truth" and "Life after Death."

The Psalmist wrote, "The heavens declare the glory of God; the sky proclaims its builder's craft. One day to the next conveys that message; one night to the next imparts that knowledge" (Psalm 19:2-3), and God gives 20/20 spiritual sight to anyone who chooses to see. The Hebrew prophet Elisha is an example.

Ben-hadad, the Syrian king, wanted Elisha's head. His army hunted Elisha across Israel before they found the prophet in Dothan. When Elisha and his servant looked across the horizon, they saw the Syrians massed everywhere against them.

"Alas," his servant called out, "what shall we do?"

Elisha knew what to do. With eyes of faith, he looked beyond the horizon to the tens of thousands of heaven's angels surrounding the Syrians. Though the physical evidence remained unchanged – the ground groaned under the weight of Syria's army – the *spiritual* evidence of impending deliverance changed fear to an assurance of victory (2 Kings 6).

When we recite, "The Almighty, maker of heaven and earth, of all that is seen and unseen," we remind ourselves that, although our physical eyes might perceive His existence, our spiritual eyes perceive His power, love, and protection. Yes. We can see a lot just by looking.

Prayer: *Open my eyes, Lord. I want to see You. I want to look into Your glory until the things of earth grow dim in the light of Your majesty and grace. Amen.*

Creed Statement: We believe in one Lord, Jesus Christ...

Today's focus: **One Lord**

And now, Israel, what does the Lord, your God, ask of you but to fear the Lord, your God, and follow his ways exactly, to love and serve the Lord, your God, with all your heart and all your soul, to keep the commandments and statutes of the Lord (Deuteronomy 12:12-13).

My friend Jim knows about serving two masters. He's a middle-manager in a large defense-related industry. When his company experienced a series of consolidations and mergers, loosely associated departments absorbed entire divisions. Lines of authority were cut and rearranged. Jim now works directly for one boss, but indirectly for another. Both have sizeable influence in Jim's semi-annual and annual evaluations.

The convoluted organizational chart usually works well, but every so often Jim gets caught between the proverbial rock and a hard place when his direct line supervisor assigns him a deadline conflicting with one from his indirect supervisor.

Fortunately, Jim has always been able to persuade both supervisors to compromise. But not many people would want the 65-hour workweek those compromises usually require.

Compromise is often a useful business strategy. But for the Christian, when the issue is living a holy lifestyle, the Lord Jesus warned us a long time ago: "No one can serve two masters."

Twenty-year-old Nathan faced that difficult dilemma. He'd just hired on at an Internet-related communications business. Making better than fifty thousand dollars, with a full benefits package, the barely-out-of-high-school computer-programmer thought he'd won the lottery. But after he received his first two paychecks, his supervisor assigned him an unexpected task: debug one of their online pornography web pages.

It caught him off guard. He had no idea his company trafficked in smut. He struggled with the decision he knew he needed to make: compromise his walk with Christ and keep his salary – or walk away.

He walked away.

"We believe in one Lord – Jesus Christ." When Christ's commandments conflict with our desires, there's no room for compromise. When Christ directs us in one direction, and our employer in another, there's no room for compromise.

The prophet Elijah challenged Israel many years ago: If the Lord is God, then follow Him. If Baal, then follow him (1 Kings 18). Elijah's challenge rings through the centuries. When we repeat the Creed, we remind ourselves we have decided to follow Jesus. We will not turn back. We will not compromise.

Prayer: *Lord, I want to love You, strengthen my love. I want to obey You. Strengthen my resolve. And where I am unwilling to follow You, make me willing to be willing, to go where You want me to go. Amen.*

❧

Creed Statement: We believe in one Lord, Jesus Christ...

Today's focus: **Jesus Christ**

[Mary] turned around and saw Jesus there, but did not know it was Jesus. Jesus said to her, "Woman, why are you weeping? Whom are you looking for?" She thought it was the gardener... (John 20:14-15).

I'm such a light sleeper, I need "white-noise" to get a good night's rest. That's why I've slept with a box fan at my side of the bed for years.

As I meditated on today's focus – Jesus Christ – I wondered how often His Name becomes white-noise in my spiritual ears. I hear His Name so often, my subconscious mind sometimes reduces it to just another word in my vocabulary, like "the" or "and."

Jesus.

Christ.

The early Church recognized something extraordinary about that Name which many of us may have forgotten, or perhaps never learned: There is no other name under heaven given among men whereby we must be saved (Acts 4); prayers find their answer in that Name (John 14); the sick find healing through that Name (James 5); demons tremble at the sound of that Name (James 2); at his Name every knee will bow and every tongue confess He is Lord (Philippians 2).

The New Testament uses dozens of synonyms to describe Him: Lamb of God, Son of God, Anointed One, Shepherd, Bread of Life, Alpha and Omega, King, Savior, Messiah, Prince of Peace... And that Name has inspired men and women for two thousand years to live – and if necessary, die – for love of His Name.

So, why do people use the holy Name of Jesus as the punch line of a joke, or to voice surprise or anger, or to use as a swear word?

I have a theory: Satan understands there is eternal life in no other than Jesus. He knows forgiveness of sin is available through no other than Jesus. There is deliverance from his infernal grasp through no other than Jesus.

If the devil can delude people to believe Jesus Christ is the stuff of jokes and swear words, they won't be so quick to believe He is Son of God, Lamb of God, Great Shepherd, and Light from Light.

When we say Jesus' name in the Creed, and in reverential conversation, we join our hearts with all those in that great Communion of Saints. And we, too, have the same privilege as they: to fall to our knees in homage to Him whose Name is above every name.

Prayer: *Holy Spirit, You spoke through the prophets. Speak also to us. Help us recognize Jesus when He calls. Help us hear above the white noise the voice of Him who loves us so much that He took our sins to Calvary's cross. Amen.*

Creed Statement: We believe in one Lord, Jesus
Christ, the only Son of God, eternally begotten of the
Father, God from God, Light from Light, true God
from true God, begotten, not made, one in being with
the Father.

Today's Focus: **God from God... one in being with
the Father**

*In the beginning was the Word, and the Word was with
God, and the Word was God. He was in the beginning with God. All things came to be through Him,
and without Him nothing came to be* (John 1:1-3).

I remember Dr. Thomas. He was one of my college
teachers who helped his class prepare for scheduled
exams. He used to walk the aisles between our desks and
review the information he expected us to know. As he spoke,
he'd sometimes pause, clear his throat or make some other
gesture to indicate what he'd just read was important. He
never actually said, "This will be on the test," but everyone
knew, when Dr. Thomas gestured, we should pay attention.

Well, almost everyone. There were always a few students with other things on their minds – and they'd get the question wrong.

From the earliest days of the Church, people mixed heresies with the doctrines handed down by the Apostles. For example, in the early 4th century a renegade priest, Arius, rejected Church teaching regarding the deity of Christ. Arius believed Jesus was not co-eternal with the Father and was, therefore, inferior to the Father.

In 325 A.D., Church leaders met in council in Nicea (modern-day Turkey) to deal with the Arian heresy. The Council leaders knew that the wrong answer to the question of Jesus' deity would inevitably spread through the Church's understanding of sin, salvation, atonement, and forgiveness. Humanity's eternal destiny was at stake.

To help the Church get the right answer, the Nicene Council responded in what I like to think of as the equivalent of clearing their throats. In this case, however, they also clapped their hands and blew a trumpet in a rising crescendo, as if to say, "Hey! Pay attention! This is really important."

So we couldn't miss the point, the Fathers gave us the correct answer *seven* times in one sentence, proclaiming Jesus is: The only son of God; eternally begotten from the Father; God from God; Light from light; True God from True God; begotten, not made; one in being with the Father.

Yet, despite the seven-fold response, some got it wrong. Some still do.

False teachers have always drawn men and women from Christian faith. That's why Christ established His Church as the "pillar and foundation of truth" (1 Timothy 3:15).

When we recite the Nicene Creed, we join our faith with historic Christian doctrine dating back to the Apostles and preserved through apostolic succession. We have the opportunity to nurture that faith born in our hearts through the Holy Spirit, and instructed by the Church.

Who is Jesus? That's an easy one, if we pay attention to the pillar and support of truth when it tells us who He is. That's one test question we don't want to get wrong.

Prayer: *Father, thank You for sending the Holy Spirit to Your Church. Help us humbly receive His instruction in things necessary for our good and for our salvation. Please protect our minds from the devil's deceptions. Amen.*

Creed Statement: Through Him all things were made.

Today's Focus: **Through Him**

For from Him and through Him and for Him are all things. To Him be glory forever. Amen
(Romans 11:36).

It's all about Jesus. Always has been. Always will be. It always should be.

I ought to think of that before I start complaining about His business. Like the Mass, for example.

My wife and I had hardly left the sanctuary Sunday morning before I groused about the service. "I wish we'd sing modern choruses instead of centuries-old hymns... I thought the priest could have made a stronger point about that Gospel passage... I'd like it better if we knelt for prayer... I wonder why..."

Then I noticed my emphasis: *I* wish. *I* thought. *I'd* like. *I* wonder. My problem became disturbingly clear: I think the Mass – even life, if I'm honest – is all about me.

Well, it's not. The Mass, and all we do before and after we come into His presence is about the One through whom all things were made - heaven, earth, mountains, seas... It's about Jesus, through whom I receive reconciliation to the Father, forgiveness and redemption.

"For by Him all things were created," wrote St. Paul, *"both in the heavens and on earth, visible and invisible, whether thrones or dominions or rulers or authorities – all things have been created through Him and for Him. . . And in Him you have been made complete... having been buried with Him in baptism, in which you were also raised up with Him through faith in the working of God, who raised Him from the dead"* (Colossians 1:16; 2:10-12 NASB).

I can't help but notice Scripture's emphasis: By *Christ;* through *Christ;* for *Christ;* in *Christ;* with *Christ.*

Not a thing in there about *me.*

Perhaps if I entered the Eucharistic Celebration centered more on Him and less on me, I wouldn't be so quick to whine. If I cultivated a deeper relationship with Christ through the week, I wouldn't be bored with that holy hour on Sunday. If I meditated on the Mass readings before I left for church, the Holy Spirit might have more kindling to spark my passion for the Mass. If I entered the sanctuary early enough to pray, my heart would be ready to worship long before the Celebration began.

When I focus on me, it's easy to find fault with the priest, the choir, the temperature, the baby crying in the back. When my focus is on Him – through whom all things were made – then all things fall into proper perspective.

Prayer: *Holy Spirit, You spoke through the prophets. Help me understand the depth of those powerful words of the Creed: Through Him, all things were made. Amen.*

Creed Statement: For us men and for our salvation He came down from heaven.

Today's Focus: **For us men** (e.g. Mankind)

Are not five sparrows sold for two small coins? Yet not one of them has escaped the notice of God. Even the hairs of your head have all been counted. Do not be afraid. You are worth more than many sparrows
(Luke 12:6-7).

According to some surveys, many of us see ourselves as little more than misplaced commas in the Novel of Life. Our existence adds nothing to the story line. That might be why 400,000 people in the United States alone attempt suicide each year. That might also be why nearly 12 million Americans routinely use illegal drugs and why millions of families have been ripped apart by divorce.

But, is that what we are, simply misplaced jots on the page of life? Do we have purpose, and does anyone care we exist?

Yes, we have great purpose, and yes, someone really does care. Our Father repeatedly tells us we are not commas, but exclamation points across the face of His creation. "For I know well the plans I have in mind for you," 'says the Lord,' "plans for your welfare, not for woe! Plans to give you a future full of hope" (Jeremiah 29:11).

The Nicene Fathers didn't pull the idea of our immeasurable value to God from the air. When they wrote, "For us men and for our salvation He came down from heaven," they synthesized God's unfathomable love for humanity from hundreds of Scripture texts, texts such as:

"For God so loved the world, that He gave His only begotten Son, that whoever believes in Him shall not perish, but have eternal life" (John 3:16 NASB).

"In this is love: not that we have loved God, but that he loved us and sent his Son as expiation [atonement] for our sins" (1 John 4:10).

"Can a mother forget her infant, be without tenderness for the child of her womb? Even should she forget, I will never forget you. See, upon the palms of my hands I have written your name; your walls are ever before me" (Isaiah 49:15, 16).

Scripture's declaration of our value to God leaps off the pages from one end of the Book to the other. We are precious to Him, and He longs to gather each of us – exclamation point by exclamation point – to Himself.

Surveys that illustrate low self-esteem reflect the fruit of Satan's oft repeated lies threaded through the media and in school classrooms: There is no God. Eternal life is a myth. We're products of accidental evolutionary forces. When we die, we're forever dead.

No wonder so many lose hope – perhaps even some in the Church who, each week, receive God's invitation to the Table.

It doesn't have to be that way. Each time we recite this section of the Creed, we can turn our backs on demon-inspired lies that rob us of joy and confidence. We can allow the words of the Creed to seep into our spirits and nurture our faith so we can live self-confidently in the assurance of God's love.

What more could our Father do to convince us of our incredible value to Him than what He did for us on Calvary?

Prayer (based on Ephesians, chapter one): *I praise You Father, because in Your great love You predestined me to be adopted as Your child through Christ. I thank You that in Him I have redemption through His blood and forgiveness of sins because of Your wonderful grace lavished on me. Help me live in confidence as Your child. Amen.*

Creed Statement: For us men and for our salvation
He came down from heaven.

Today's Focus: **For our salvation**

*Blessed be the God and Father of our Lord Jesus
Christ, who according to His great mercy has caused
us to be born again to a living hope through the resurrection of Jesus Christ from the dead… obtaining as
the outcome of your faith the salvation of your souls*
(1 Peter 1:3, 9 NASB).

S alvation, like other theological concepts, begs for definition. I've read authors who spent hundreds of pages to
illustrate and define the word, but none did so as succinctly
or powerfully as a two-year-old child illustrated it for me.

At the conclusion of a home Bible study, Berea's mother
left for a few moments to get a package from her car. When
Berea saw Mommy leave, her eyes widened in fear; she
ran to the door, stretched in vain for the knob and screamed
for her mother. I could hear the terror in her cry, as if she
believed Mommy would never return.

One of the women lifted Berea into her arms and tried
to calm her, but the child only wanted Mommy. When her
mother returned and saw Berea's nearly inconsolable grief,

she gathered her in her arms, held her close, and whispered in her ear. Almost immediately, Berea settled down, laid her head on Mommy's shoulder, and snuggled into her arms.

The words of the Creed, "For our salvation," remind us God became Man to pay the enormous debt we owed Him because of our sins. "For our salvation" means those who call out to Christ for forgiveness, seeking His mercy and warmth, will never be alone. Throughout eternity, God's children will know the strength of the Father's arms, feel His caress, and hear Him whisper, "It's okay. I'm here. I love you."

"In My Father's house are many dwelling places," the Lord Jesus promised. "If it were not so, I would have told you; for I go to prepare a place for you. If I go and prepare a place for you, I will come again and receive you to Myself, that where I am, there you may be also" (John 14:1-3, NASB).

It's not enough to define the concepts of our faith. Atonement, grace, mercy and the rest must take root in our hearts. Salvation means we are saved *from* something – saved from an eternity alone, separated from the Father because of our sins.

Can you imagine eternity without sensing the Father's care or ever hearing His whispers of love?

Two-year-old Berea taught me more about salvation in those few moments than I learned in all of my seminary training. She reminded me salvation's joy springs from knowing – really knowing – the Father will bring us to Himself and cleanse us in the blood of the Lamb. And we will forever snuggle into His arms to never, ever, be alone again.

Prayer: *Lord, restore to me the joy of Your salvation. Give me a spirit that seeks, above all else, to rest in Your arms. Forgive my sins and bring me to life eternal. Amen.*

Creed Statement: For us men and for our salvation
He came down from heaven.

Today' Focus: **He came down from heaven**

*When the queen of Sheba witnessed Solomon's great
wisdom, the palace he had built, the food at his table,
the seating of his ministers, the attendance and garb
of his waiters, his banquet service, and the (burnt
offerings) he offered in the temple of the Lord, she
was breathless* (1 Kings 10:4-5).

Never had the queen heard such wisdom as when
Solomon spoke. Never had she witnessed the opulence
and splendor she found in the Temple and in his palace.
"The report I heard in my country about your deeds and your
wisdom is true," she said to him. "Though I did not believe
the report until I came and saw with my own eyes, I have
discovered that they were not telling me the half" (I Kings
10:6-7).

We can learn something of heaven from the queen's
experience in Jerusalem.

The writers of Scripture made valiant attempts to describe heaven. Daniel saw the Lord dressed in snow bright clothing, His throne like fire (Daniel 7:9-10). St. John witnessed a golden city, clear as glass. Its gates are huge pearls; the foundations decorated with precious stones like jasper, sapphire, emerald, topaz, and amethyst. The city has no need of sun or moon, for the glory of God gives it light (Revelation 21:10-23). Isaiah saw a place where wolves and lambs graze together and lions eat straw like oxen; and "none shall hurt or destroy on all my holy mountain, says the Lord" (Isaiah 65:25).

Despite her royalty and wealth, the queen of Sheba couldn't imagine what awaited her in Jerusalem. How much less can we understand what awaits us in the place Christ is still preparing for His children (John 14:1-3)? Human language can never capture heaven's fullness. Echoing the queen of Sheba's breathless remark, St. Paul wrote: "What eye has not seen, and ear has not heard, and what has not entered the human heart, what God has prepared for those who love Him" (1 Corinthians 2:9).

Like trying to describe the melodies and crescendos of a symphony to a person born deaf, or a sunset shimmering with shades of yellow and violet to a person born blind, how can we understand heaven when all we know is earth? And how can we comprehend what Jesus experienced when He left Glory to enter humanity?

But, there's more. The Lord Jesus did not only leave heaven behind. Before His incarnation, Jesus dwelt within the Holy Trinity in a way we can never understand. When the Second Person of the Trinity clothed Himself with flesh, He somehow separated from that eternal, ineffable relationship within the Triune Godhead.

And He did it willingly – for us and for our salvation.

When Christ came from heaven to earth, He emptied Himself of His glory and clothed Himself – forever – in human form (Philippians 2:5-8; Catechism of the Catholic Church, paragraphs 659, 663). Why did the Godhead transform their eternal triune relationship? Why did Christ leave that state of unknowable splendor to feel hunger and thirst, weariness and pain, to enclose Himself in human form? Knowing that so many would reject Him, mock and blaspheme Him – even 2000 years later – why did He come?

Because He loves us.

Say the Creed quickly, and that profoundly personal truth loses something fundamentally sacred. Mull it over in context with what we know of heaven and Calvary, and John 3:16 soars to new heights of meaning: "For God so loved the world that he gave his only Son, so that everyone who believes in him might not perish but might have eternal life."

"He came down from heaven." Think of it! He who was rich beyond imagination became poor for our sakes, that we might share his eternal wealth (2 Corinthians 8:9).

Oh, Hallelujah! What a Savior.

Prayer: *Lord Jesus, I owed a debt I could never pay. You left Glory to pay a debt You never owed. Because of Your payment, I am now free. Thank You, dear Lord. Thank You. Amen.*

Creed Statement: By the power of the Holy Spirit He was born of the Virgin Mary...

Today's Focus: **By the power of the Holy Spirit**

The Holy Spirit will come upon you, and the power of the Most High will overshadow you. Therefore the child to be born will be called holy, the Son of God... for nothing will be impossible for God
(Luke 1:35-37).

Is anything too difficult for the Third Person of the Trinity? Of course not. He does whatever He wants, whenever and however He wants. Nothing and no one is outside His control, and few Christians question the reach of His power.

But the more I read and study about the Holy Spirit, the greater the danger that He becomes little more than an academic concept – the object of catechism classes and homilies, creeds and Scripture study.

He should be more. He must be more. He is more.

I thought about His Being one morning as I read the opening verses of Genesis where we first meet the Him:

"In the beginning God created the heavens and the earth. The earth was formless and void, and darkness was over the surface of the deep, and the Spirit of God was moving over the surface of the waters. Then God said..." (Genesis 1:1-3 NASB).

I usually move past this portion of text and into the six days of creation without so much as a thought about the personal application of those first three verses. After all, what does the awe-inspiring panorama of Creation have to do with *me*?

Plenty.

"In the beginning" takes us back to the first moments of Earth's birth, a time when chaos reigned. And darkness. And emptiness.

I've known those feelings – chaos, darkness, and emptiness. I've fallen many times to my knees in despair as private chaos swirled around me. I've hunted for something solid to grasp hold of in the midst of a roiling cauldron. I've longed for direction and instruction in palpable darkness.

That's not an easy place to be – surrounded by confusion and chaos. Yet, in retrospect, I've learned it's a good place to be, because when my resources have vanished and my strength is gone, I'm more willing to do what I should have done in the beginning – quiet myself, let the Holy Spirit move over the surface of my confusion until the Father says, "Let there be light. And peace. And fullness."

In the thirty-three years I've served Him, He has never failed to bring peace into my chaos, be an anchor in my storm, and cast light into my darkness.

But that shouldn't surprise me. After all, God never fails any of His children.

Never.

Prayer (of St. Augustine): *Breathe in me, Holy Spirit, that all my thoughts may be holy. Act in me, Holy Spirit, that my work too may be holy. Draw my heart, Holy Spirit, that I may love only what is holy. Strengthen me, Holy Spirit, to defend all that is holy. Guard me, Holy Spirit, that I may always be holy. Amen.*

Creed Statement: By the power of the Holy Spirit He was born of the Virgin Mary…

Today's focus: **He was born**

Behold, the virgin shall be with child and bear a son, and they shall name Him Emmanuel, which means "God is with us" (Matthew 1:23).

I remember our excitement when my wife, Nancy, and I learned she was pregnant with our first child. It happened more than thirty years ago, but the memories remain vivid. We waited with growing anticipation during the nine months as Nancy's abdomen slowly expanded. We watched in awe as her belly rippled when Keren stretched in the womb. We busied ourselves with planning and shopping and decorating long before we brought our baby home.

Our daughter was born March 12, 1977, in a warm and hygienic hospital delivery room. The obstetrician handed Keren to a nurse, who wiped her clean with a soft towel, wrapped her in a blanket, and laid her in a warm bassinet.

The pediatrician examined our daughter and, a few minutes later, the nurse carried her to Nancy's arms.

What loving parent doesn't hope their children will enter the world snuggled in a warm blanket, laid in a comfortable bed, and watched over by an adoring family? What mom or dad doesn't long to wrap their children in soft clothing and give them colorful toys?

If anyone might have expected that kind of experience, Mary and Joseph probably did. After all, the Virgin carried the Son of God within her womb, conceived through the miraculous intervention of the Holy Spirit.

Babies just don't get any more special.

But when His parents arrived in Bethlehem, the town was already swollen with strangers. Joseph and Mary, tired and hungry from their journey, longed for a place to bathe and a bed to let their weariness give way to refreshing sleep. Instead, Joseph searched in vain for a clean and comfortable place for his wife to lie down. They settled for the night with cattle and to the smell of manure and rotting straw.

To make an uncomfortable situation worse, Mary went into labor.

Why did God bring His son into the world in a barn instead of a manicured palace? Why did He permit His Son to be born far from family and friends who could nurture the Infant and help the new mother care for Him?

I don't know. That's not the way I'd have done it. But were I to guess, I'd say it happened that way so God could demonstrate from the very beginning of His work for our salvation that "Emmanuel" really does mean God is with us – in our poverty, complete with rotting straw, manure and flies.

The Creed reminds us Jesus was born as most of humanity is born: in humble surroundings with the most meager of necessities. Christ knows the fullness of our harshest experiences because He lived through them – from a feeding trough to a splintered cross, with the Via Dolorosa – the Way of Suffering – between the two.

Jesus' birth – like His life – is God's assurance that He is intimately connected to our humanness. He understands our loneliness, our sorrow, our confusion. And through it all, He remains only a prayer away from drawing us to Himself, wrapping us in His arms and wiping us clean with His blood.

Prayer: *Father of the Lord Jesus Christ, when I am rushed and confused, compose and quiet me. Make my heart like a comforted child, not looking at my circumstances, but always to You, my shelter, my anchor, my peace. Amen.*

Creed Statement: By the power of the Holy Spirit He
was born of the Virgin Mary…

Today's Focus: **The Virgin**

*And Mary said: "My soul proclaims the greatness of
the Lord; my spirit rejoices in God my savior. For He
has looked upon his handmaid's lowliness; behold,
from now on will all ages call me blessed"*
(Luke 1:46-48).

W hy did God choose Mary to bear His Son? What did
He see in her that moved Him to select the Virgin
to nurture, comfort, and educate the Savior of the world?
We don't know. Scripture is silent. But we can infer several
reasons from what Scripture *does* tell us.

First, Mary possessed courage. In first century Israel,
unmarried pregnant girls were outcasts. Israelite culture
considered sexual immorality a capital offense, punishable
by stoning. That's why the adulterous woman in St. John's
gospel (chapter 8) would have died had Jesus not intervened.
Mary, knowing her unwed pregnancy would cost her reputa-

tion, probably her betrothal to Joseph, and perhaps even her life – nevertheless, laid herself at God's feet and told the angel, "Be it done to me according to Your word."

And Mary knew Scripture. In an era when catechists didn't consider it a priority to teach Scripture to girls, it's clear Mary read and memorized God's word. Her adoration of God (Luke 1:46-55) is an example of her scripture knowledge. She quotes or alludes to at least six Old Testament texts in those short eleven verses (1 Samuel 2:1-10, Psalm 34:2, Psalm 35:9, Psalm 98:1, Psalm 103:17, Psalm 107:9). Mary applied what the Psalmist declared centuries earlier, "Your word is a lamp for my feet, a light for my path" (Psalm 119:105).

Mary also demonstrated humility. She could have told the angel, "You're asking too much of me. Send someone else." But instead, she answered, "May it be done to me..." In other words, she said not her will, but God's. Not her plans, but His. Perhaps as she spoke, she remembered Solomon's conclusion in Ecclesiastes, "The last word, when all is heard: Fear God and keep his commandments" (Ecclesiastes 12:13). Perhaps she remembered the Proverb, "Charm is deceptive and beauty fleeting; the woman who fears the Lord is to be praised" (Proverbs 31:30).

Further, Mary presented herself obedient to God. "Behold, I am the handmaid of the Lord." If Eve, the Mother of mankind, had answered God as Mary, and not disobeyed the Father's commandment about the forbidden tree, salvation history would be different. But Eve disobeyed; and Mary, by her obedience, fixed what our first mother broke.

And Mary proved herself chaste. "For from the heart," the Lord Jesus said, "come evil thoughts, murder, adultery, unchastity, theft, false witness, blasphemy. These are what defile a person..." (Matthew 15:19-20). Mary knew none of these. She was a virgin not only in flesh but also in spirit.

And finally, if there is a final word about the Mother of God, Mary didn't model herself after the world, but let love for God transform her into a useful vessel for Him. No wonder He chose her to carry and mother His Son. When we recite, "He was born of the Virgin Mary," we remind ourselves to imitate her, to clothe ourselves with obedience, humility, courage, purity, and knowledge of God's word. God chose Mary to bring Christ *into* the world. By imitating Jesus' mother, we bring Him *to* our world.

Prayer: *Holy Mary, Mother of God, pray for us sinners, that we will learn to love God with all our heart, soul, mind and strength. Amen.*

Creed Statement: By the power of the Holy Spirit He was born of the Virgin Mary, and became man.

Today's focus: **He became man**

So Jesus came out, wearing the crown of thorns and the purple cloak. And (Pilate) said to them, "Behold, the man!" (John 19:5)

At unexpected times, my memory's eye catches glimpses of my deceased father. I see him in myself when I'm lost in thought and absently rub my fingers the way he used to. I see him sit ramrod straight when I hold my shoulders as he did. I see him in the mirror when I hold my chin a certain way to shave. His movements and patterns remain ingrained in my subconscious long after his death. But that I see him so often in myself shouldn't surprise me. Children typically imprint some of their parents' characteristics.

What kind of man was Jesus? How did He live and what were His habits? We do well to answer these questions because in learning to imitate Christ, we imprint His Father's characteristics onto our subconscious and grow more closely into the image of God (2 Corinthians 3:18).

So, who was Jesus?

He was a Man of prayer. St. Luke wrote, "But the news about Him was spreading even farther, and large crowds were gathering to hear Him and to be healed of their sicknesses. But Jesus Himself would often slip away to the wilderness and pray" (Luke 5:15-16 NASB).

He was compassionate. "At the sight of the crowds," St. Matthew records, "His heart was moved with pity for them because they were troubled and abandoned, like sheep without a shepherd" (Matthew 9:36).

He possessed an intimate knowledge of the Scriptures. He quoted as easily from Moses as from the Prophets, from the Psalms to the Writings.

He was passionate for holiness. "Take these out of here," He commanded the moneychangers. He turned over their tables, tossed their coins across the floor, and chased them from the temple. "Stop making My Father's house a market-place" (John 2:16).

And He was a Man of humility. How can we understand the eternal Second Person of the Trinity, clothed in the flesh of a man, and yet He washed His disciples' feet?

When we recite the Creed and focus on God who became Man, we can take the opportunity to meditate on His life of prayer, holiness, humility, compassion, and knowledge of Scripture. And by meditating, we can learn to imitate Him who fully reflects the Father.

Prayer: *Holy Spirit, make me as a child in my Father's arms. Open my eyes to observe Christ's life, His habits, His passions. Imprint those things on my heart that I may walk as He walked. Amen.*

Creed Statement: For our sake He was crucified under Pontius Pilate...

Today's Focus: **Crucified under Pontius Pilate**

When Pilate heard these words he brought Jesus out and seated Him on the judge's bench in the place called Stone Pavement, in Hebrew, Gabbatha... Then he handed Him over to them to be crucified
(John 19:13,16).

When my wife was five, she discovered who killed Jesus.

"I positioned the pointed end of a bobby pin against Mom's hand," Nancy said. She thought if she nailed her mother to the bed she wouldn't get up and take care of the new baby. She'd have Mommy all to herself.

"Pound, Pound," she said as she tapped the bobby pin with her fist.

Her mother woke with a start and grabbed the pin from Nancy's hand. "What are you doing?" her mom shouted. "That's what people did to Jesus."

Her face suddenly flushed with shame, Nancy ran to her bedroom, hid beneath her blanket and sobbed. She remembers the guilt that flooded over her. "I was only five, but I wondered if I was like the people who nailed Jesus to the cross. I loved Jesus. I'd never do anything to hurt Him."

Who killed Jesus?

It's easy to cast blame for Jesus' death on first century religious and political leaders. But when we do, we miss the point of the crucifixion. We miss the reason God sent His Son as the atonement for our sins.

The Hebrew prophet Isaiah wrote: "He was pierced for our offenses, crushed for our sins, upon Him was the chastisement that makes us whole, by his stripes we were healed.... the Lord laid upon Him the guilt of us all" (Isaiah 53:5, 6).

St. Paul told us Christ was handed over for our transgressions (Romans 4:25), and, "Our old self was crucified with Him, so that our sinful body might be done away with, that we might no longer be in slavery to sin" (Romans 6:6).

Long before my wife learned the theology of sin and salvation, she knew intuitively as a kindergartner what many adults go to their grave never learning. The Jews didn't kill Jesus. Pilate and the Romans didn't kill Him.

We did.

Our sins killed the holy Son of God as surely as if we ourselves hammered the spikes into His hands and jabbed the spear into His side.

The words of the Creed, "He was crucified under Pontius Pilate," invite us to remember the Roman governor was not the only one responsible for Jesus' death. Our sins whipped His back and pressed thorns into His forehead. Our sins nailed Him to that splintered cross. In the timelessness of God's eternity, we were there when they crucified the Lord. We were there when they laid Him in the tomb.

And we were there when He prayed, "Father, forgive them, for they know not what they do."

Prayer: *Lord Jesus, I am so sorry my sins nailed You to that cross. Forgive me. Show me the depth of my sin, that I might understand the depth of Your love. Lead me to deeper repentance and more faithful obedience. Amen.*

Creed Statement: He suffered, died, and was buried.

Today's Focus: **He suffered**

From that time on, Jesus began to show his disciples that He must go to Jerusalem and suffer greatly from the elders, the chief priests, and the scribes, and be killed and on the third day be raised
(Matthew 16:21).

It began with flogging. Roman soldiers on either side of Christ swung whips embedded with metal and bone against his back. Every blow ripped open new strips of skin until his muscles and tendons quivered in a mass of bleeding flesh. Most prisoners died of shock long before they were nailed to the cross.

After the beating, the soldiers forced Jesus to drag his cross to Calvary where they laid it on the ground and threw Him down onto it. Soldiers mocked the Lord of Glory as they hammered spikes through His wrists and feet, tearing through flesh, blood vessels, and nerves.

As He hung between heaven and earth, breathing became an all-consuming struggle. Gravity restricted His respiratory muscles, forcing Him to push against his feet and flex His arms just to breathe. But that intensified the strain on the ravaged nerves in his wrists, and each breath forced His swollen back against the splintered wood. Every movement, every moment on the cross, inflamed His physical torment.

But that was not all Christ endured. He also suffered immeasurable spiritual loneliness. "My God, my God," Jesus cried aloud. "Why hast thou forsaken me?" In that brief moment (what a moment it must have been for the eternal Son of God), when He, "who did not know sin," became Sin for us (2 Corinthians 5:21), the Father turned His back on His Son for the first time in *eternity*.

Why did Jesus do it? Why did Almighty God empty Himself of infinite glory, clothe Himself in inglorious flesh, and permit vicious men to beat Him, spit on Him, pull out His beard, and nail Him to a cross? Why did He become "sin for us"?

The Creed reminds us why. He did it for our sake. If Jesus had not taken our sins to the cross, then we – you and I – would suffer the eternal consequences our sins deserved. If not for Christ's redemptive death that paid the penalty our sins required from a holy God, then *we* would be the ones to eventually – and inevitably – hear at the Judgment, "Depart from me, you evildoers" (Matthew 7:23).

If I say the Creed too quickly, I run the risk of missing the depth of significance Jesus' suffering means for me. I risk brushing past the gravity of my sin when I fail to contemplate the magnitude of my mutiny against God's authority. When I recite the Creed, and look at the crucifix above the altar, I remind myself that the Lord Jesus would not have suffered Calvary's agony if there'd been another way to purchase my salvation.

But there was no other way. The thrice-holy God of the prophet Isaiah's vision (Isaiah 6) demands my holiness. Nothing short of death could satisfy God's judgment of my sin. And nothing short of Christ's sacrificial atonement could satisfy God's mercy to pardon my sin.

Why did Jesus suffer for our sake? Because – and we can't hear this too many times – because He loves us. He immeasurably, unfathomably, undeservedly loves us.

Prayer: *Lord, I do not understand the full weight of my sin. Holy Spirit, please, I beg You, reveal to my heart the magnitude of my rebellion that I might love Christ the more for dying in my place. Amen.*

Creed Statement: He suffered, died, and was buried.

Today's Focus: **Died, and was buried**

Now faith is the assurance of things hoped for, the conviction of things not seen...

(Hebrews 11:1 NASB).

This was not simply disappointment. It was gut-wrenching tragedy. Their hopes for freedom from Roman tyranny lay stained with blood at their feet. Their confidence in a future of peace was nailed with Him to a splintered cross. Grief threatened to smother them. The Virgin cradled her Son's head and wept. The disciples beat their breasts and mourned their teacher and friend.

Cruelty and death seemed victorious. Desperation reigned.

It's a familiar and personal story for many of us. Who hasn't experienced the death of hope, a wounded spirit, or haunting despair? Like ashes on the tongue, who hasn't known failure, self-doubt and the endless litany of "what-ifs"? Children drift from the faith as they become adults.

Marriages fail. Addictions bind loved ones in shackles stronger than those that held the demoniac (Mark 5:1-4). And we look at heaven and wonder if God knows we're alive. Or if He cares.

When devilish doubts pierce my faith, I try to focus on Calvary because that mournful hill reminds me Friday looks darkest before Resurrection Sunday.

Jesus did so much more than simply die on that cross. His death proved God's faithfulness to His many promises in Scripture to send a Savior. As early as Genesis 3:15, the Father promised the human family a Redeemer, someone to free us from the Serpent's grasp, to take "captivity captive." On Friday, Satan bruised God's heel. On Resurrection Sunday, God crushed Satan's head.

Jesus' death ripped apart sin's impenetrable barrier that separated us from God. The prophet Isaiah wrote, "Your iniquities have made a separation between you and your God and your sins have hid His face from you, so that He does not hear" (Isaiah 59:2 NASB). But on that Friday, God shattered the barrier. Laying our sins on Christ's shoulders (Isaiah 53:5, 6), the Father threw open the gates of reconciliation (2 Corinthians 5:19).

Jesus' death proved God's love for us. It's easy to skim over John 3:16 and not sense the searing emotions the Father suffered as He watched His Son agonize on Calvary. But when we meditate on Christ's scourging, the spikes, and His wounds, we can better understand the passion behind the meaning of that verse – God so loved *me*, that He gave His Son.

Jesus' death clothed us with righteousness. The harlot, the thief, murderer, adulterer... think of it! There is no sin that cannot be cleansed by Christ's blood. There is no penitent sinner who cannot be made as righteous before God's eyes as Jesus Himself (1 Corinthians 1:30; 2 Corinthians 5:21).

Finally – if there can be a final point about Christ's death – the Savior's death challenges us to repentance. When the crowd in Jerusalem (Acts 2:22-41) learned it was *their* sins that nailed Christ to the cross, "they were cut to the heart." In unison they cried, "Brethren, what shall we do?" St. Peter responded, "Repent," and three thousand were baptized and added to the Church.

Jesus' death seemed the end of hope to those gathered around the cross because no one knew Sunday was coming. But you and I know better. When we recite, "He suffered, died, and was buried," we remind ourselves God knows us, God cares...

And Sunday is coming.

Prayer: *Lord Jesus, I know Sunday is coming, but the time between Friday and Sunday sometimes seems so terribly long. Give me grace to wait in faith, to trust that You, who began the good work in us and in those we love, will complete it. Amen.*

Creed Statement: On the third day He rose again in fulfillment of the Scriptures...

Today's focus: **He rose again**

But now Christ has been raised from the dead, the firstfruits of those who have fallen asleep
(1 Corinthians 15:20).

During the summer of 2005, I led a Children's Liturgy of the Word. Each week I had the privilege to teach seven and eight-year-olds the wonders of our Catholic faith. We studied Scripture and Church teaching about such holy mysteries as the Trinity, the Incarnation, Resurrection, Christ's atonement, and His Presence in the Eucharist.

Where some adults who've heard the stories for decades might nod off to sleep, children's eyes grow wide with wonder. Where some adults hesitate with doubt, children receive the ancient truths with uncomplicated faith.

I met one of those children in my class. The second-grader had been told, "People killed Jesus, and He's dead."

He shared this information in a low, somber voice, glancing at me once or twice, and then dropping his gaze to the floor. I bent and looked into his face. "Yes," I said. "Some people killed Jesus. But three days later, He came back to life. He is alive. Right now. Today." I emphasized the word, "Today."

I hope I'll never forget the child's face. His eyes suddenly glistened. His countenance lifted. He straightened his shoulders as if a weight had been removed, pumped his arm, and shouted, "Yes!"

No wonder the Lord Jesus said, "Amen, I say to you, unless you turn and become like children, you will not enter the kingdom of heaven" (Matthew 18:3). That youngster's faith is something every adult in the Church would do well to emulate.

St. Paul proclaimed, "If there is no resurrection of the dead, then neither has Christ been raised. And if Christ has not been raised, then empty [too] is our preaching; empty, too, your faith" (1 Corinthians 15:13-14).

The Apostle continued, "Behold, I tell you a mystery. We... will all be changed, in an instant, in the blink of an eye, at the last trumpet. For the trumpet will sound, the dead will be raised incorruptible, and we shall be changed... [and] then the word that is written shall come about: 'Death is swallowed up in victory. Where, O death, is your victory? Where, O death, is your sting?'" (1 Corinthians 15:50-55).

The bodily resurrection of Christ is the linchpin – the cornerstone – of Christianity. No wonder liberal theologians, philosophers, and teachers have, for two thousand years, attacked the Resurrection. Destroy it, and Christianity loses its authority to declare Christ alone is the door to eternal life, that no one comes to the Father except through Him. Destroy the Resurrection and we have no assurance of forgiveness of sin. If Jesus died and that was the end of it, then the

Communion of Saints, Christ's Presence in the Eucharist, and our hope of heaven is all a farce.

Yet, this is the glorious truth you and I are privileged to proclaim each week when we profess our certainty that Christ died and was buried...

And on the third day, rose from the grave.

If that doesn't stir something inside us to shout, "Hallelujah," if that incredible reality doesn't move us to a holy awe – the maybe we should check *our* pulses.

Prayer: *Lord Jesus, with child-like faith, I believe in Your resurrection. Have mercy on me and permit me to share eternal life with Mary, the virgin Mother of God, the apostles, and all the saints who have done Your will throughout the ages. Amen.*

Creed Statement: On the third day He rose again in fulfillment of the Scriptures...

Today's Focus: **The Scriptures**

But you, remain faithful to what you have learned and believed, because you know from whom you learned it, and that from infancy you have known (the) sacred scriptures, which are capable of giving you wisdom for salvation through faith in Christ Jesus. All scripture is inspired by God and is useful for teaching, for refutation, for correction, and for training in righteousness, so that one who belongs to God may be competent, equipped for every good work
(2 Timothy 3:14-17).

The Church has always taught that God is the author of the Scriptures. That's why she venerates Scripture as she venerates the Lord's Body (Catechism of the Catholic Church, paragraphs 103, 105). St. Gregory the Great, called the Bible, "A letter from Almighty God to His creatures." St.

Jerome admonished, "Ignorance of Scripture is ignorance of Christ."

But some people are not so sure.

Like Jason.

"How do we know the Bible is God's word?" Jason interrupted my lesson.

My high school catechism class had been studying St. Paul's letter to the Colossians, but his question caught the interest of the other teens in the class. I sensed we needed to take a detour from St. Paul's letter.

"Well," I answered, "What's your definition of God?"

He scrunched his forehead and asked what I meant.

"Is God omnipotent?" I looked at the others, inviting them to consider my question, too. "Is He all-powerful? Can He do whatever He wants, whenever He wants, however He wants?"

Jason shrugged. "Sure."

"Is God omniscient? Does He know everything about everything? There aren't any mysteries to Him?"

Jason nodded.

"What about omnipresence? Is God everywhere at every moment? Is He in this classroom and, at the same time, in France, India, and Mexico?"

He nodded again.

"One more question," I said. "Is God a loving God?"

"Uh-huh," he agreed.

"Are you sure?"

"Yeah."

"Okay. Let's work backwards. If God is a loving God, then we can expect Him to want to communicate with those He loves, right?"

I smiled and walked closer to Jason.

"Since God loves us, and He is all-powerful – how difficult do you think it would be for Him to ensure His message is accurately transmitted across the centuries? Since He is all-knowing, He knows the best way to communicate with us, and because He is everywhere at the same time, He can simultaneously speak to anyone who reads His Word with an open heart."

I walked back to the lectern and took the Bible in my hand. "That's one reason an ancient Israelite king said, 'Trust in the Lord, your God, and you will be found firm. Trust in his prophets and you will succeed. ' And St. Paul added, 'See to it that no one captivate you with an empty, seductive philosophy according to human tradition, according to the elemental powers of the world and not according to Christ'" (2 Chronicles 20:20 and Colossians 2:8).

I looked at the students and wondered if I was making sense to them. My reasons for believing the inerrancy of God's word might not have satisfied Jason and the others, but rehearsing those reasons reminded me once again why the Church teaches us we can trust the Bible to be the unfailing and inerrant word of God. When we recite, "in fulfillment of the Scriptures," we can stand confident of God's commitment to guide us to salvation through the inspired words of Scripture. For good reason, the Catechism urges us "to learn 'the surpassing knowledge of Jesus Christ,' by frequently reading God's word" (Paragraph 133).

Prayer: *Lord, Your word is a lamp to my feet and a light to my path. Teach me Your ways and I will walk in Your truth. Amen.*

Creed Statement: He ascended into heaven and is
seated at the right hand of the Father.

Today's Focus: **He ascended into heaven**

*While meeting with them, He enjoined them not to
depart from Jerusalem... but you will receive power
when the Holy Spirit comes upon you, and you will
be my witnesses in Jerusalem, throughout Judea and
Samaria, and to the ends of the earth." When He had
said this, as they were looking on, He was lifted up,
and a cloud took Him from their sight*
(Acts 1:4, 8, 9).

Terror smothered the disciples' joy like a thick, wet
blanket when the soldiers captured Jesus in the Garden.
They fled before they, too, could be led away with their Lord.
Peter, following at a safe distance, denied three times that he
knew his best friend.

None of the disciples knew it at the time, but their
emotional roller coaster was just beginning. When Pilate
crucified the Lord, their hopes died – only to rekindle three

days later to Mary Magdalene's, "He's risen! He's alive!" Their hope collapsed again when they found the tomb empty.

When the Lord appeared in the upper room, hope soared once more – and then plummeted forty days later as they watched Him leave.

Do you know about emotional rides? As I've said before in these meditations, I know how it feels to scan heaven in vain for answers to prayer. I know what it's like, even in the midst of what should be a glorious celebration of the Mass, to fixate on my family losses, broken relationships, or financial reversals.

I'd do much better to focus instead on the miraculous event taking place before my eyes as bread and wine transform into His body and blood. I should drop to my knees in awe and in reverence as He appears before me. I should fix my eyes on Jesus, "the author and perfecter of faith" (Hebrews 12:2, NASB).

What must it have been like for the disciples to fix their eyes on Christ as He ascended, to see earth lose its hold on Him? What were they thinking? If I'd been there, I'd have wondered how I could go on.

When we recite, "He ascended into heaven," God gives us opportunity – especially during times of loneliness and sorrow – to go on. He beckons us to look with eyes of faith to the heavens, from where our help comes. The Holy Spirit trades our emotional derailment for His encouragement, our loss for His sufficiency, our defeat for His victory.

That's a critically important point, and we should take care not to miss it. Sorrows, overwhelming as they may be, last only for a time, but the shout of victory is ours come morning (Psalm 30:5). Just as earth's gravity could no more hold Christ than death could, sorrows hold us only to the extent we give them permission.

He is risen. He is ascended. He is sitting – now, at this moment – at the Father's right hand. Unless and until we look beyond the bottom of our ride, we won't recognize the *personal* significance of Christ's ascension to the Father. We'll settle for emotional derailment and defeat instead of the victory we have in the risen and ascended Savior.

"Lift up your heads, O gates, and be lifted up, O ancient doors, that the King of glory may come in!" (Psalm 24:7, NASB).

Prayer: *Hallelujah to the crucified One. Glory to the risen One. Adoration to the ascended One. Who is like You, Oh, Lord? Perfect in majesty, ever in unity with the Father and the Holy Spirit and ever present at our right hand. Amen.*

Creed Statement: He ascended into heaven and is seated at the right hand of the Father.

Today's Focus: **He... is seated at the right hand of the Father.**

Therefore . . let us also lay aside every encumbrance and the sin which so easily entangles us, and let us run with endurance the race that is set before us, fixing our eyes on Jesus, the author and perfecter of faith, who for the joy set before Him endured the cross, despising the shame, and has sat down at the right hand of the throne of God
(Hebrews 12:1-2 NASB).

I don't remember his name. Mike, I think. But I remember the last time I saw him. It was nearly 40 years ago. I was standing on a street corner when his mom stopped at a red light. Mike sat in the passenger seat. He and I graduated high school the year before. I'd not seen him since.

"Hey, Mike!" I smiled and walked toward the car while the light was still red. "How're you doing? Haven't seen you in...".

The rest of the words stuck in my throat as I glanced at his legs. The right was missing. Amputated just above the knee.

"Wh- what happened?" I stuttered.

"Vietnam."

The light turned green and I muttered something like, "Oh, wow," as they pulled away.

It's not hard for me to imagine the sorrow Mike's parents have endured these many years for their son. I now have three grown children and I know how I'd feel if any were so horribly wounded. When Mike and his parents sat at the dinner table, or watched television, or went for a drive, they had only to glance in his direction and see his missing leg. For the rest of their lives, their son's wound will remind them of war's horror.

Scripture speaks with somber regularity of our involvement in a lethal spiritual war (for example, 2 Corinthians 10, Ephesians 6, the Book of Revelation). We know the Lord Jesus was a casualty of that war; He was wounded, suffered, and died. But when He rose from the dead, the Glorious One ascended to His rightful place on His kingly throne. The Righteous One's death reconciled us to the Father. The Wounded One purchased our lives with His holy blood.

Although the grief of parents for their children cannot compare with the sorrow of the Divine Father for His Son, as a father myself, I can begin to imagine the eternal Father's sadness each time He sees His Son's wounds. The lacerations from thorns pressed into His forehead, the slices of the whip across his back, the punctures of nails and lance – they remain ever-present marks of the spiritual war in which Jesus gave His life so we would not face eternal death.

I don't know if Mike's parents take comfort knowing their son suffered so others might be free. But Scripture tells us the heavenly Father is pleased to know His Son's suffering brought us freedom from Satan's grasp (Isaiah 53).

America awards the Purple Heart to its military wounded in battle. But what shall Jesus receive for His wounds? What mark of thanks could properly honor His sacrifice? What jewels could adequately acclaim His worthiness?

The only award worthy of His sacrifice is that we give Him our heart, soul, mind and strength. Each time we recite the words of the Creed, "Christ is seated at the right hand of the Father," we have the privilege to do just that.

Prayer (from St. Ignatius of Loyola): *Lord, teach us to fight and not heed our wounds, to toil and not seek rest, to labor and not ask for reward except that of knowing that we do Your will. Amen.*

Creed Statement: He will come again in glory to judge the living and the dead...

Today's Focus: **He will come again**

And if I go and prepare a place for you, I will come back again and take you to Myself, so that where I am you also may be (John 14:3).

It shouldn't have surprised me. For two weeks, the highway department had posted notices that they planned to resurface the asphalt, fill the potholes, and smooth the roadway. As far as I was concerned, they couldn't fix the road soon enough. I'd slammed into the craters so many times my teeth were loose.

I suppose it's because I saw the notices each day that I stopped paying attention to them. Before long, the signs blended into the background as I swerved down the street, trying not to crack the front axle. So, when I left the house that morning and turned the corner, the unusually smooth ride startled me. For the first time in months, the mini-van didn't rattle. I didn't dodge potholes or worry about losing my teeth. When I stopped for the traffic light at the next corner, I noticed even my palms were dry.

Asphalt highways are not the only places ravaged by potholes. Many of us slam into craters along life's highway. Heartaches jar us to the roots of our teeth. Failures break our confidence.

Then one day we see notices posted along the path. One promises, *The rough places will be made smooth* (Isaiah 40); another promises, *In the twinkling of an eye we shall be caught up to be with the Lord* (1 Corinthians 15); and, *I will come again and receive you to Myself* (John 14), declares a third.

There are so many declarations we have to slow down to read them all. Over and over, season after season, we hear them. We talk about them. We debate their meaning. Before long, they become old friends.

And that could become a problem for us. Perhaps because the promises grow so familiar, we stop paying attention. The signs get lost in the busy-ness of punching time clocks, fighting traffic, washing clothes, paying overdue bills... We focus so much on dodging potholes, we no longer remember the promise that one day all who belong to Christ will leave the house, turn the corner – and find the road paved.

When we recite the words of the Creed, "He will come again," we remind ourselves to not become complacent or grow weary in waiting. We remind ourselves to focus instead on Scripture's unshakable promise – Christ will come again. And when He returns, He will caress every grieving heart and embrace every splintered life with His eternal love. Never again will we worry about rough roads.

Sometimes I think it can't happen soon enough.

Prayer: *Come quickly, Lord Jesus. We long for Your appearance. Make us faithful in our journey that we may gather in Your presence with joy. Amen.*

Creed Statement: He will come again in glory to judge the living and the dead...

Today's Focus: **In glory to judge the living and the dead**

I saw.... one like a son of man, wearing an ankle-length robe, with a gold sash around his chest. The hair of his head was as white as white wool or as snow, and his eyes were like a fiery flame. His feet were like polished brass refined in a furnace, and his voice was like the sound of rushing water.... A sharp two-edged sword came out of his mouth, and his face shone like the sun at its brightest. When I caught sight of Him, I fell down at his feet as though dead (Revelation 1:12-17).

Of all the images I've ever seen of Jesus, none inspired fear. The Baby in a manger, the Man feeding the 5,000, or even the One hanging on a cross inspired a blend of serenity, confidence, and yes, sorrow.

But never fear; and that's unfortunate.

I've known about Christ for decades. I've read the gospels dozens of times. In the thirty years since my conversion to Christianity, I've heard thousands of sermons about Him, taught classes about Him, written hundreds of articles about Him. But I'm not sure the Jesus of my intellect – perhaps even of my faith – has prepared me for the Jesus of glorious reality.

That seems to have been the Apostle John's experience. If anyone knew Christ, St. John did. For three years the Beloved Apostle ate with the Lord, walked with Him, listened to Him teach. He was among Christ's closest friends. It was to St. John, standing at the foot of the cross, that Jesus committed the care of the Blessed Mother.

Yet, the Jesus that John knew was not the same Jesus he met on the Isle of Patmos (Revelation 1). You might remember the story. When the apostle saw the glorified Christ, he fell on his face as a dead man.

Have you ever wondered what it will be like to see Jesus in His glory? Will we raise our voices in hallelujahs, or put our hands to our mouths in reverent and holy awe? Will we stand before Him in exulted adoration, or fall before his feet as dead?

Two thousand years ago, Jesus entered history as a lamb: meek, humble. But when He comes again, it will not be as a lamb. With His eyes afire, a sword flashing from His mouth, and His face radiant as the sun, Christ will come as King to judge the living and the dead (See Revelation 1).

The certainty of His return in glory should give all of us pause. It should cause us to review our lifestyles and evaluate our priorities. Christ was serious when He told his followers, "Not everyone who says to me, 'Lord, Lord,' will enter the kingdom of heaven, but only the one who does the will of my Father in heaven" (Matthew 7:21). Surely that is why St. John cautioned Christ's followers to live properly so that we would not shrink from Him at His appearing (1 John 2:28).

"He will come again in glory to judge the living and the dead." When we recite those words, we remind ourselves that God gives us plenteous opportunities to find pardon in the Sacrament of Reconciliation. We have abundant opportunities to receive Christ's divine life in the Sacrament of the Eucharist.

And we ought to take those opportunities seriously.

We might today know *about* Christ, but one day we will see Him as He really is – in all of His glory. Surely, we don't want to live in such a way that we shrink from Him when He appears.

Prayer: *Lord, more than anything else, I want to be faithful. I want the words of my mouth and the meditations of my heart to always please You. Soften my heart to Your voice. Quicken my mind to obedience. Direct my passions toward Your service. Amen.*

Creed Statement: He will come again in glory to judge the living and the dead, and His kingdom will have no end.

Today's Focus: **His kingdom**

As the visions during the night continued, I saw One like a son of man coming, on the clouds of heaven; When He reached the Ancient One and was presented before Him, He received dominion, glory, and kingship; nations and peoples of every language serve Him. His dominion is an everlasting dominion that shall not be taken away, his kingship shall not be destroyed (Daniel 7:13-14).

Ramses the Second, one of ancient Egypt's greatest pharaohs, reigned over an area from present-day Iraq to the Sudan. During his 67-year rule, Egypt enjoyed unsurpassed military might and economic power. Today, the ruins of his kingdom give silent witness to his prominence in the ancient world.

But time has a way of leveling even the greatest rulers. When archaeologists unearthed the ancient king and sent his mummified body to the Cairo Museum, a befuddled tax inspector, not sure what to label the shriveled corpse taxed it as imported dried fish.

"Man in his pomp," the Psalmist wrote, "yet without understanding, is like the beasts that perish" (Psalm 49:20, NASB). Despite our schemes and dreams, calendar pages fall one by one like leaves shaken by an autumn wind. Time breathes across our names and reputations until all that remains are crumbling artifacts.

Egypt, Israel, Babylon, Greece and Rome – they're the stuff of textbooks and museum relics. Their pharaohs, emperors, and kings invested their energies to make names for themselves, and yet today are as relevant as – well, as dried fish.

I can easily presume the lessons of the worthlessness of wealth, and the inevitable transience of empires, applies only to the rich and powerful. That would be an erroneous presumption. My attitudes toward others could benefit from a humble recognition that, five hundred years from today, my name will also have as much relevance as that of Ramses'.

No wonder St. Paul wrote: "Have among yourselves the same attitude that is also yours in Christ Jesus, who... emptied Himself, taking the form of a slave..." (Philippians 2:5-7). No wonder the Psalmist warned us to number our days and apply our hearts to wisdom (Psalm 90:12). That wisdom tells us only one King will live into eternity. Only one Kingdom will never end.

When we recite, "His Kingdom will have no end," we remind ourselves that our personal fiefdoms are like vapors in the wind. Knowing that, how then ought we to live? How shall we walk except in humility before God and our neighbors? When the last leaf has fallen to the dirt, only those who committed themselves and their resources to *His* kingdom will hear what every child of God hopes to hear at the Judgment: "Well done, my good and faithful servant. Since you were faithful in small matters, I will give you great responsibilities. Come, share your master's joy" (Matthew 25:21).

Prayer (from Pope Clement XI and the Psalmist): *Help me to know this world is passing, that my true future is the happiness of heaven, that life on earth is short, and the life to come eternal. Teach me to number my days, that I might apply myself wisdom. Amen.*

Creed Statement: We believe in the Holy Spirit, the Lord, the giver of Life...

Today's Focus: **The Holy Spirit**

For all who are being led by the Spirit of God, these are sons of God. For you have not received a spirit of slavery leading to fear again, but you have received a spirit of adoption as sons by which we cry out, "Abba! Father!" The Spirit Himself testifies with our spirit that we are children of God...
(Romans 8:14-16 NASB).

It's easy for me to remember the heavenly Father. I repeat His name each morning when I say the "Our Father." I focus on Him through the day when I petition Him for others and myself. And, when I listen – which doesn't happen as often as it should – His commandments come to mind when I'm tempted to stray from the narrow path of holiness.

His Son, Jesus, is also easy to remember. I see artistic representations of Him in prints around my home. I wear His image on a crucifix around my neck. He is the central theme of the altar at each Mass.

But, dare I admit it? The Holy Spirit, the third Person of the Trinity, is easy to forget. Forgive me, Lord.

Though I affirm my belief in Him when I recite the Creed, and I'm intellectually aware of His existence, somehow He gets lost in my religious world of rituals, liturgies, rote prayers and Scripture study. Drawings of Him as a dove alighting on Jesus at His baptism, or as tongues of fire on the one hundred and twenty in the upper room don't help me focus on the Holy Spirit's *Being* and His indispensable role in my life.

As I write these words, I shake my head to realize how spiritually blind I can be.

The Holy Spirit is my comforter, even when I'm not aware that it is He who quiets my anguished heart. When I doubt the Father's love, He stirs confidence and unspeakable wonder within my spirit, affirming that I really *am* His child. When I stumble into sin, He prompts me to prayer, repentance, and holiness.

It is the Holy Spirit who creates in me a hunger to know Jesus far beyond form and ritual. When I listen to or read Scripture, it is the Holy Spirit who illuminates truth in my mind where otherwise I would grope in darkness. It is He who gives me direction as I struggle to know God's will for my life.

It is He who heals my broken relationships, broken body, and broken mind.

"We believe in the Holy Spirit." It's good for me to recite those words of the Creed. Each time I do, I remind myself of His magnificent, compassionate, and passionate Presence with me – with us. He is our Comforter, Guide, Deliverer, Advocate, Intercessor, Teacher, and Friend.

We would all do well not to forget that.

Prayer: *Come, Dove of heaven, Fire of the Father, Breath of God, Power of God, Intercessor before God, God at my right hand. Come, Lord. We need You. Amen.*

Creed Statement: We believe in the Holy Spirit, the Lord, the giver of Life...

Today's Focus: **Giver of Life**

Prophesy over these bones and say to them, 'O dry bones, hear the word of the LORD.' Thus says the Lord GOD to these bones, 'Behold, I will cause breath to enter you that you may come to life. 'I will put sinews on you, make flesh grow back on you, cover you with skin and put breath in you that you may come alive; and you will know that I am the Lord
(Ezekiel 37:4-6 NASB).

Yom Kippur is the holiest of the Jewish holidays. It's the day Jews set aside to fast and pray for God's mercy. In 1972, I spent that day alone in my navy barracks, feeling unusually remorseful. I remembered what I'd done a year earlier, on that same holy day. I'd been in bed with one of my girlfriends.

I typically avoided thinking about sin – especially my own. I'd always dismissed those thoughts with rationalizations about how good I was when compared to others. But on that holiest of days in the Jewish calendar, I reviewed my life and saw nothing but sexual immorality, drunkenness, thefts, and blasphemies. As I sat at my desk, staring out the barracks window, I anguished over what I could do. I wouldn't promise God I'd not sin anymore. I dared not compound my dark past with a promise of future obedience – a promise I knew I wouldn't keep.

In despair, I walked to my locker, pulled my journal from the top shelf, settled back onto the chair and wrote, "God, forgive me for my past sins, and look with tolerance on my future ones."

That was the best I could think of – ask God to be tolerant of my future sins. I knew I'd never change because I was hopelessly trapped in a cycle of doing right and doing wrong. If I'd known St. Paul's lament, I'd have cried to God with the same passion, "For the good that I want, I do not do, but I practice the very evil that I do not want... Wretched man that I am! Who will set me free from the body of this death?" (Romans 7:19, 24 NASB)

Who, indeed?

Two months later, during the Christmas season, a co-worker offered me a book about Bible prophecy. As I made my way through the short chapters, I learned about Jesus, the Jewish Messiah, who died on Calvary to pay the penalty God requires of everyone who departs from God's laws. And I learned Christ's sacrificial atonement brought forgiveness for my sins.

All of them.

In December 1972, I didn't know about priests and sacraments. I knew nothing about Church doctrines and salvation. I only knew I was a sinner – and I was grief-stricken over my sins. I bowed my knees beside my bed, looked toward heaven and said, "God, I'm sorry for the way I'm living. I'm sorry for my sins. Jesus, please forgive me. Wash my sins in Your blood."

Thunder didn't roll at my "Amen." Lights didn't flash. A weight didn't lift from my shoulders. But in that moment of confession, I sensed the Giver of Life – the Holy Spirit – breathe life into my dry bones. Before I got off my knees, I knew what I needed to do: be baptized and seek to obey God for the rest of my life. Old things had passed away. Everything was now new (2 Corinthians 5:17).

When we recite, "We believe in the Holy Spirit, the Lord, the giver of Life," we have the opportunity to affirm – and reaffirm – it is only the Holy Spirit who guides us into truth (John 14:26). He alone breathes life into our spirits. He alone walks beside us to comfort and heal our hurts (Acts 9:31). And He alone opens our spiritual eyes to see and our spiritual ears to hear the Savior.

Prayer: *Come, Holy Spirit, we need You. Open our eyes to see Jesus. Open our ears to listen, and our hearts to repent of our sins and obey Your Word. Amen.*

Creed Statement: We believe in the Holy Spirit, the Lord, the giver of Life, who proceeds from the Father and the Son.

Today's Focus: **Who proceeds from the Father and the Son**

When the Advocate comes whom I will send you from the Father, the Spirit of truth that proceeds from the Father, He will testify to me (John 15:26).

A foreboding pressure – like an ominous presence – spread over me. It pressed like a suffocating weight across my chest and abdomen. I tried to push it away, but my arms wouldn't move. I wanted to scream, but couldn't open my mouth. I heaved, trying to force air through my lips. But my body refused to respond. Again and again, until terror overwhelmed me. In a final, frantic lunge, I exploded with a shattering, guttural cry.

That woke me.

I stared at the LCD screen on my clock. 6:10. I was grateful for the morning, but stayed in bed until my breathing slowed. When I finally stumbled into the living room for my usual start-the-day time with Jesus, I slipped a CD into the player, put on earphones and tried to lose myself in worship. But the night terrors lingered in the back of my mind.

For many of us, life is sometimes like a nightmare from which we can't awaken. Loved ones fall seriously ill and, despite our prayers, suffer and die. Families shatter. Victories hover just beyond our reach. Claustrophobia rises in our throat. We call for help, but can't force air past our lips.

And then, like awakening from a bad dream, God's light explodes through our darkness. The Holy Spirit illuminates His presence with us as we read a passage of Scripture, hear a hymn, or someone speaks God's word to us. In that moment, God's assurances become tangible. The Holy Spirit whispers, "Come to me, all you who labor and are burdened, and I will give you rest. Take my yoke upon you and learn from me, for I am meek and humble of heart; and you will find rest for yourselves. For my yoke is easy, and my burden light" (Matthew 11:28-30). Our spiritual ears grab hold of the Spirit's encouragement, "Trust in the Lord with all your heart, on your own intelligence rely not; In all your ways be mindful of him, and he will make straight your paths" (Proverbs 3:5).

The Paraclete (from the Greek, meaning advocate, counselor, helper, comforter) proceeds from the Father who loves us so much that He gave his only Son to die so we might live with Him forever. The Paraclete proceeds from the Son who, because of His great mercy, became our sin and bore our death penalty (2 Corinthians 5:21, Isaiah 53).

The Psalmist wrote, "Where can I go from Your Spirit? Or where can I flee from thy presence?" (Psalm 139:7 NASB). To the farthest ends of the earth, and in our loneliest moments, the Holy Spirit surrounds us. Bone to bone, and flesh upon flesh, He formed us in our mother's womb and set our hearts beating before we took our first breath.

So intimate is He with us, He knows our thoughts before we speak them, and what's on our hearts even before we know they're there. When we recite the Creed, "He proceeds from the Father and the Son," we remind ourselves that whatever our nightmare, the Holy Spirit's light pierces our darkness. Whatever our sorrow, He is our comfort. Whatever our confusion, He is our counselor. Whatever our need, He is our helper.

Prayer: *Come to us, Holy Spirit. We desperately need You. Be light in darkness, our guide in waywardness, our teacher in our ignorance. We would not flee from Your Presence. We would instead run toward it. Accept us in our search for You. Amen.*

Creed Statement: With the Father and the Son, He is worshiped and glorified.

Today's Focus: **He is worshiped and glorified**

The grace of the Lord Jesus Christ and the love of God and the fellowship of the Holy Spirit be with all of you (2 Corinthians 13:13).

I know why St. John used the Greek word, Paraclete, to describe the Holy Spirit. The word's range of meaning – advocate, comforter, helper – illuminates His relationship with us.

The Advocate pleads for us before the Holy Tribunal of God. The Comforter touches our wounded hearts as no other can comfort. He is our help when we grow weary with the battle. With so many doctrinal opinions competing for our attention, the Holy Spirit guides us though the Church into truth and protects us from error.

What I *don't* understand is why some try to dilute the Third Person of the Holy Trinity to an "it" or an impersonal "force" – unworthy of the same worship given the Father and the Son.

That was Macedonius' problem. The 4th century bishop rejected the Holy Spirit's deity, and Church leaders recognized his heretical views posed a grave threat to Christian faith. In 381 A.D., they met in Constantinople for the Second Ecumenical Council where they authoritatively defined the doctrine of the Trinity. The Council amended the earlier Nicene Creed (of 325 A.D.) to include: "We believe in the Holy Spirit... who proceeds from the Father and the Son. With the Father and Son, He is worshiped and glorified."

Macedonius was wrong about the Holy Spirit. But, as I reflected on the words, "With the Father and Son, He is worshiped and glorified," I realized – even though I know better – I sometimes don't give Him the same place in my heart as I do the Father and the Son. In the three decades I've been a Christian, I've asked the Holy Spirit for guidance, pleaded with Him to empower me for service, and begged Him to draw my loved ones to the Savior. Yet, I have never said, "Holy Spirit, I love You. I adore You. I worship You." Even as I pray, "Glory be to the Father, and to the Son, and to the Holy Spirit," my tongue forms the words that honor the Holy Spirit, but my mind lingers on the Father and Son.

Why?

I suppose it's because, after all these years, I still have trouble transforming intellectual understanding into spiritual reality. I still find it easier to focus on the Father and the Son than on the ethereal third Person of the Trinity.

When I declare with the rest of the congregation, the Holy Spirit is worshiped and glorified – unless my affirmation moves twelve inches from my head to my heart, I risk becoming like many first century Church-goers who had a form of godliness but denied its power (2 Timothy 3:5).

That's not what I want. And that's not what the Holy Spirit wants.

Prayer: *Holy Spirit, forgive us for unconsciously reducing Your glory, majesty, and authority. Help us worship You as we worship the Father and Son because You are worthy of the same adulation. Make me – make the Church – passionate in seeking You, the giver of life and the source of truth. Amen.*

Creed Statement: He has spoken through the prophets.

Today's Focus: **He has spoken through the prophets**

For this reason we also constantly thank God that when you received the word of God which you heard from us, you accepted it not as the word of men, but for what it really is, the word of God, which also performs its work in you who believe
(1 Thessalonians 2:13).

Walter, a nursing assistant on my staff, was in the middle of his complaint when I entered the room. "Life has no purpose," he said.

I slipped into my seat at the table where the rest of the day crew waited for the night nurse to join us for change-of-shift report.

"It's meaningless," he continued. "We live, and then we die."

I'm not usually at a loss for words, but this time was different. I knew Walter claimed to be an atheist, but I puzzled why a 20-year-old man held such somber sentiments about life. By the time I recovered enough to introduce my opinion into the gloom hovering about us, the night nurse breezed through the door, sat down and began the summary of her patients. I held my tongue – and kicked myself for letting the opportunity with Walter slip by.

As her report wound to a close, the door behind me opened. Without looking up, I knew it was the hospital chaplain. He joined us each morning for a brief reading of Scripture and prayer. He took his seat behind me and waited for the nurse to conclude. When she stood to leave, I invited those who wanted to stay for the meditation to remain. As I expected, Walter left.

"I had planned to read something else," Chaplain Bernard started, "but earlier this morning, I decided to share thoughts about this passage, instead."

I recognized Psalm 139 as soon as he started reading. I shifted in my chair and stared at him, keenly aware God had orchestrated the change of his text.

"O Lord, You have searched me and known me. You know when I sit down and when I rise up; You understand my thought from afar. You scrutinize my path and my lying down, and are intimately acquainted with all my ways. . . If I ascend to heaven, You are there; If I make my bed in Sheol, behold, You are there. If I take the wings of the dawn, if I dwell in the remotest part of the sea, even there Your hand will lead me, and Your right hand will lay hold of me... You formed my inward parts; You wove me in my mother's womb" (Psalm 139:1-3, 8-10, 13 NASB).

The silence that followed when he closed the Bible and finished his prayer lasted only a moment. It seemed like a week. Finally, another nursing assistant said, "It's too bad Walter wasn't here to hear that."

I regret that he, and those who left the room with him, didn't hear the Holy Spirit's response to Walter's desperate world-view. Life *does* have purpose – because the Triune God has a personal hand in our lives.

But, I wonder if it would have mattered to Walter.

Throughout history, the Holy Spirit has spoken to humanity through His prophets and apostles. But for those like Walter who reject the supernatural or scoff at the idea that God communicates through Scripture, the words of the prophets and apostles are no different from the words we read in our newspaper.

It's no wonder the Walters of the world think life has no purpose or hope.

When we recite: "We believe in the Holy Spirit... He has spoken through the prophets," we do more than express our conviction that the words of Scripture are divinely inspired. We confess our confidence that the Holy Spirit still speaks through those same prophets and apostles, and that His words give all who believe hope in despair, guidance in confusion, peace in turmoil.

Prayer: *Holy Spirit, I believe You spoke through the prophets. Increase my faith to believe You speak to me through the Scriptures. Increase my sensitivity to Your voice and my obedience to follow You into truth. Amen.*

Creed Statement: We believe in one holy catholic and apostolic Church.

Today's Focus: **Holy**

I urge you therefore, brothers, by the mercies of God, to offer your bodies as a living sacrifice, holy and pleasing to God, your spiritual worship
(Romans 12:1).

My son was driving slowly toward our house when I spotted the broken bottles near our driveway.

"Go around them," I said. "You don't want to risk a flat tire."

Although Zion was a student driver, I hadn't expected him to take me literally. Instead of easing the car around the glass shards, he turned left at the corner and continued around the block. A few minutes later, we returned to the house, approaching now from the opposite side of the street.

At the time, I couldn't speak for fear I might laugh out loud. But for months afterward, he and I joked about his half-mile detour.

As time passed, I forgot the incident. Then I heard about Eric and Lynn. Their story reminded me of how important it is to go out of our way to avoid damaging our spiritual tires.

Eric and Lynn worked for a computer supply manufacturer. Lynn was shy; Eric, energetic and personable. She was quiet. He had a sense of humor that left her sides aching from laughter. Though attracted to him, Lynn decided not to see Eric socially because he didn't attend church. Nevertheless, they spent considerable time together during the workweek.

At first, they talked business. As time passed, their conversations shifted focus. He began asking questions about her faith. Lynn looked forward to their daily conversations.

Three months later, he dropped a bombshell. "I'm married," he told her.

Lynn strained to control her emotions. In the time they'd known each other, he never hinted he had a family. A week later, he offered to rent an apartment for them in the city.

Lynn knew the right thing to do, but knowing right and doing right do not always coincide. Her emotional attachment to Eric had grown nearly out of control. Her mind and her heart pulled in opposite directions. Days dragged into weeks as Eric continued to woo her.

Lynn knew she was in trouble, so she prayed. She asked others to pray. Finally, she recognized the serious threat her relationship with Eric would have on her relationship with Christ. She quit her job, moved and unlisted her phone.

When we recite, "One holy… Church," we remind ourselves, and each other, that God calls the Church – you and me – to holy lifestyles. Lynn learned what all mature Christians discover: holiness doesn't just happen. It requires effort, and that effort sometimes comes with great emotional and financial cost.

Who doesn't have a spiritual Achilles' heel? For good reason, Scripture warns us to flee temptation, to go out of our way to avoid situations that can leave us with flat tires and stranded on our journey toward His kingdom (1 Timothy 2:22). Mature Christians know life is more fragile – and eternally more valuable – than steel-belted radials.

Prayer: *Holy Spirit, sanctify my mind and my heart. Make me persevere in holiness. Fix my eyes on Jesus and help me cleanse myself from every defilement of body and spirit. Amen.*

Creed statement: We believe in one holy catholic and apostolic Church.

Today's Focus: **Catholic and apostolic church**

I am writing you about these matters, although I hope to visit you soon. But if I should be delayed, you should know how to behave in the household of God, which is the church of the living God, the pillar and foundation of truth (1 Timothy 3:14,15).

The emergency occurred more than 15 years ago. Yet, it surfaces in my memory as if it occurred last week. I was the Charge Nurse in the intensive care unit, and as I made my rounds through the area, I heard the ominous sound of gurgling lungs from a patient's room. I walked toward her bed, assessed the critical situation, and called other staff to the room. "Get me some oxygen," I barked at one person. "Start an IV," I told another. "Get me some suction," I ordered a third.

But, it was the respiratory technician's reaction that stopped me in mid-sentence. He told me the patient didn't need to be suctioned.

"Excuse me?"

"I don't think she needs suctioning," he repeated.

Meanwhile, my team of nurses scrambled to prevent the patient from spiraling into respiratory and cardiac arrest. With as much self-control as I could gather, I said, "Stop arguing and suction the patient, or I'll do it myself."

He stared at me, as if trying to decide what to do. Finally, he huffed his annoyance and set up his equipment. As soon as he snaked the tube along the patient's trachea, thick yellow secretions slurped into the collection canister. Within moments, the patient relaxed and her vital signs stabilized.

Authority. I hope that technician learned the importance of authority that evening. Without a legitimate chain of command – whether in hospitals, or factories, in city governments or families – good outcomes become the exception instead of the rule.

A legitimate chain of authority is no less important in the Church, yet, how many Catholics reject lifestyle or doctrinal declarations by Church leadership? For example, although Rome has repeatedly declared its position on artificial birth control, divorce and abortion, some in our pews openly, or tacitly, oppose those teachings.

The Church declares Christ is physically present in the Eucharist, yet one recent survey found 60% of Catholics don't believe that to be true. The Church admonishes the faithful to avoid the occult, yet many Catholics read books or watch movies that glorify wizardry, sorcery and other occult themes.

Christ commissioned the Church to bring healing to a spiritually sick humanity. The Charge Nurse – Christ – is calling for suction, but many of us stand around and argue with that decision.

Meanwhile, societies and cultures are drowning in their secretions.

When we recite, "We believe in one holy, catholic and apostolic church," we affirm our conviction that God gave to the leadership of His Church – leadership stretching back in an unbroken line to the apostles – the exclusive authority to define doctrine and teach the faithful how to live out their faith.

When we recite the Creed, we affirm our intention to obey the Church's legitimate authority. Otherwise, how can we hope to successfully fulfill the Great Commission to rescue the perishing?

Prayer (from the Act of Faith): *O God, help me practice the truths You have revealed through Your Church. I am sorry for exalting my opinions above the clear teaching of those You appointed over us. Forgive me. Help me walk in better obedience.*

Creed Statement: We acknowledge one baptism for the forgiveness of sins.

Today's Focus: **Baptism**

Corresponding to that, baptism now saves you – not the removal of dirt from the flesh, but an appeal to God for a good conscience – through the resurrection of Jesus Christ... (1 Peter 3:21 NASB).

Odie is our family dog. Well, more accurately, Odie is my wife's dog. I tolerate the mutt only because Nancy loves him.

It's not that our mixed Pug/Chihuahua is bad. It's just that he has no sense of hygiene. We could bathe him every day, but as soon as we let him out of the house, he'll find a spot where another dog has marked its territory, and rub his coat against it.

The thought of petting Odie after he's been outside gives me goose bumps. Even after I've touched him to attach his leash, I keep my hand at arm's length until I find soap and hot water.

Nancy tells me I'm being silly. "He's a dog," she says. "That's what dogs do." Well, that might be what dogs do, but that doesn't mean I have to touch him after he's done it.

Between you and me, I'm glad I'm not a dog snooping around in other dogs' business, and every now and then, like the Pharisee in the eighteenth chapter of St. Luke's gospel, I thank God I'm not like other people who roll around in dirt.

That's when the Holy Spirit reminds me how often I sniff the bushes.

When I watch television shows or movies that Jesus wouldn't watch, I'm snuggling up to garbage. When my eyes linger on things I shouldn't see, I'm rubbing against putrefied trash. When I boast of "my" accomplishments, "my" talents, "my" skills, instead of giving honor to the One who permits me to take even my next breath, I'm wallowing in mud.

I don't like to admit it, but I need a spiritual bath more often than I think I do.

When we recite, "We acknowledge one baptism for the forgiveness of sins," we remind ourselves why we were baptized – to wash away our sins and be born of God (John 3:3-7). When we presented ourselves in Christian faith for baptism (or our parents presented us) we trusted the blood of Jesus to atone for our sins (1 John 1:7) and vowed to obey God the rest of our days. When the priest baptized us in the name of the Father, the Son and the Holy Spirit, we didn't just get wet. We got cleansed. God took us from the kennel and put us into His family.

But there's more. When we dip our fingers into the baptismal font before Mass and anoint ourselves with holy water, we have the extraordinary opportunity to remind ourselves of that supernatural Sacrament. We have the extraordinary privilege to then enter the sanctuary, kneel at our pews with our foreheads still wet, and renew our solemn pledge to God to avoid sin and the near-occasion of it.

For good reason, Scripture warns against forgetting those vows, of becoming complacent in our walk of faith, of acting like a dog that "returns to his own vomit" or a sow, which, "after washing, returns to wallowing in the mire" (2 Peter 2:22).

Our faith and baptism made us children of God. The Father expects us to behave like it.

Prayer: *Lord, I was buried with You in my baptism and was raised with You to live a holy life. Help me consecrate myself to You today – and every day. Help me avoid attitudes and actions that displease You. Amen.*

Creed Statement: We acknowledge one baptism for the forgiveness of sins.

Today's Focus: **Forgiveness of sins**

While he was still a long way off, his father caught sight of him, and was filled with compassion. He ran to his son, embraced him and kissed him. His son said to him, 'Father, I have sinned against heaven and against you; I no longer deserve to be called your son.' But his father said... we must celebrate and rejoice, because (he) was dead and has come to life again; he was lost and has been found
(Luke 15:20-22, 32).

I didn't intend to eavesdrop. I doubt they even noticed me as I leaned against the wall. The family focused too closely on their private ordeal to pay attention to anyone else in the airport terminal.

When they reached the row of seats across from me, they stopped. The young woman lowered her travel bag to the floor.

"There's still time to change your mind," her father said softly.

The daughter, probably in her early twenties, nodded and turned toward the glass wall. Her plane waited at the gate. "Call us when you get settled," Mom said, breaking the tension. "Let us know how you are."

Mom and Dad looked at each other. Both tried to smile. Dad slipped his hands into his pockets and stared at the passing crowd. A few moments later, a voice broke over the loudspeaker, "We will now board rows 20 through 28. Please have your boarding passes ready for the agent at the door."

"Well," Dad sighed as he put his arm around her shoulder and pulled her close. "Take care of yourself." His voice caught. "Call if you need anything. Come home whenever you want."

She brushed a kiss to his cheek, hugged her mother, looked once more at her father – and walked away.

Why was she leaving? How long would she be gone? I don't know any more about the family than what I overheard and saw during that brief interlude at the terminal gate. What I *do* know, however, is perhaps the most important part of the story. Mom and Dad wanted her to stay. Even to the last moment, before boarding the plane, they hoped she would change her mind – and they made sure to remind her she would always be welcomed home.

As they watched their daughter disappear down the corridor toward her plane, my heart suddenly caught a sense of another Parent's pathos, and I wondered, how often does the heavenly Father stand before one of His children and plead, "I wish you wouldn't go"? And how many return an awkward smile – and walk down the corridor of self-righteousness, sexual immorality, greed, and other sins?

"For the forgiveness of sins." When we recite this portion of the Creed, we proclaim our confidence that God will forgive every penitent sinner, regardless of the transgression – or its frequency. No sin is too dark, no violation of His Law too deep that Christ's blood cannot purify and the Sacrament of Reconciliation can't bring pardon. Calvary still echoes with God's plea to His wayward children, "Turn from your rebellions and come home." Again and again He says it: "Come home."

Why does anyone stray down the corridor of rebellion when it breaks the Father's heart to see us walk away?

Prayer: *Lord Jesus, You said, there is more joy in heaven over one sinner who repents, than ninety-nine who need no repentance. Lord, I have sinned and I am sorry. Forgive me, for Christ's sake, and restore to me the joy of Your salvation. Amen.*

Creed Statement: We look for the resurrection of the dead...

Today's Focus: **The Resurrection**

Martha said to Him, "I know he will rise, in the resurrection on the last day." Jesus told her, "I am the resurrection and the life; whoever believes in me, even if he dies, will live, and everyone who lives and believes in me will never die. Do you believe this?" (John 11:24-26).

As soon as I walked into the hospital room, I knew my friend was dying. Six weeks earlier, Dan's doctors diagnosed his colon cancer. Then they found a tumor in his left lung and suspicious spots on his liver.

"Hi Dan," I choked back tears and tried not to notice his labored breathing or his yellowed, swollen skin.

"How are you feeling?"

He opened his sunken eyes and tried to smile.

"Tired," he whispered. "Good to see you."

It had been nearly five years since we'd last seen each other. My job change and move across country had ended our weekly sit-down-over-coffee chats. When we spoke on the phone nine months earlier in December, no one knew it would be his last earthly celebration of Christ's birth.

I watched him struggle for air, and my mind drifted to his conversion story. He'd been raised an agnostic by agnostic, culturally Jewish parents. He was educated in prestigious schools and trained as a clinical psychologist, and could have easily dismissed the emptiness gnawing at his heart as irrational foolishness. The idea that sin could be the root of his void was as distant to his humanistic worldview as light is from darkness.

But when the Holy Spirit revealed to him the truth about sin, forgiveness and salvation, Dan knew he had to make a choice: bow to God or continue hiding behind human philosophies.

He chose God, and devoted his life to the cornerstone of God's truth – Jesus Christ.

Twenty-two years later, although cancer weakened his body, it couldn't weaken his faith. Everyone who walked into his room heard the same question, "Do you know my Jesus? Do you know my Savior?"

The next day when I visited again, I asked, "Dan, how does it feel to know you're dying?"

I wanted to know my friend's thoughts as he faced eternity. I'd learned from experience that a hospital room is one of those places where everything we hold dear slips to the bottom of our priority list: money, popularity, passions, careers. Like charred timbers after a house fire, a deathbed places so many things in clearer perspective. I thought Dan's answer might help me cope during that time when I also stare into eternity.

He raised his hand to the bed-rail and touched mine.

"From life to life." He smiled. "I leave this one to enter the next with Jesus. I fought the good fight. I finished my course. I kept the faith."

We buried Dan a few weeks later. A chilled November wind whipped across the southwest Missouri cemetery. Rust-orange leaves carpeted the frozen dirt at our feet, and as the eulogy drifted from the graveside, Dan's final words to me filtered again into my memory, "Life to life. I leave this one to enter the next with Jesus."

"We look for the resurrection of the dead," because for those who love Jesus, death is not the end. It's the beginning of eternity with the Savior. Christ unites those who've died in communion with Him to join in one majestic hymn of praise around His throne.

When we recite the Creed we ask the question – and at the same time shout our response: Death, where is your victory? Grave, where is your sting? It was trounced, and forever crushed when the stone rolled away and Jesus walked from the tomb.

Hallelujah!

Prayer: *Lord Jesus Christ, dying, You destroyed our death. Rising, You restored our life. Oh, Lord, come in glory and bring us to everlasting life. Amen.*

Creed Statement: We look for the resurrection of the dead, and the life of the world to come.

Today's Focus: **Life of the world to come**

Then I saw a new heaven and a new earth. The former heaven and the former earth had passed away, and the sea was no more.... I heard a loud voice from the throne saying, "Behold, God's dwelling is with the human race. He will dwell with them and... He will wipe every tear from their eyes, and there shall be no more death or mourning, wailing or pain, (for) the old order has passed away" (Revelation 21:1, 3, 4).

I'm glad this section of the Creed links "the resurrection of the dead" with "the life of the world to come." It reminds me I will reunite with those I've loved, who are now on the other side of the grave.

One of them is my baby – my baby whom I killed.

I was seventeen when my girlfriend told me she was pregnant. I knew Judith expected me to propose marriage. Instead, I told her to get an abortion.

I remember how nonchalantly I passed sentence on our child. I chose to believe the life growing inside her womb was nothing more than a glob of cells. That's what pro-abortion activists called it, and I eagerly accepted their lies because I didn't want to be inconvenienced with a baby.

I lived with that awful guilt for many years – until I found solace in Christ forgiveness and hope in Scripture's promises. Two of those promises in particular brought peace to my spirit: "If we confess our sins, He is faithful and righteous to forgive us our sins and to cleanse us from all unrighteousness" (1 John 1:9 NASB); and, "In Him we have redemption through His blood, the forgiveness of our trespasses, according to the riches of His grace which He lavished on us" (Ephesians 1:7, 8 NASB).

Though my terrible sadness lingered, I could rest in the assurance that God forgave me for killing my baby.

However, thirty-three years after becoming a Protestant Christian, the Holy Spirit deepened my comfort when He led me home to the Catholic Church and I learned the full meaning of the Communion of Saints. The Church's teaching of that Communion assures me that my baby, killed before she took her first breath, is in heaven because of God's abundant mercy – *and* that she is praying for me.

And that she forgives me.

Oh, what solace is that thought; She forgives me.

I choose to believe my baby was a girl. I've named her Celeste. My daughter, whom I never got to hold, is alive in that "world to come," and when we meet, she will wipe the tears that still flow when I think of my cruelty and selfishness.

When Christians repeat those inestimable words of promise: "We look for the resurrection of the dead and the life of the world to come," we can take great comfort in knowing that those who wait for us around God's throne – even those we hurt in this life – forgive us. Washed in the blood of the

Lamb and now perfected in love, they wait to welcome us to a world without death, grief, or tears. In that place, there is only forgiveness, tenderness, and love. Amen.

Prayer: *Lord, comfort us in our grief as we remember loved ones and friends who have gone before us. Help us look with joyous anticipation for the resurrection of the dead and the life of the world to come. Amen.*

Creed Statement: Amen.

Today's Focus: **Amen**

*Consider it all joy, my brothers, when you encounter
various trials, for you know that the testing of your
faith produces perseverance* (James 1:2-3).

"We believe... We believe... We believe..." The
ancient summary of Christian faith flows from
my tongue like a poem's comfortable and regular meter. I
recite declaration of faith after declaration, each as important as the last, none more necessary than the next – not
even (it would seem) the "Amen" at the end of the Creed.
But that should not be the case. I don't think there is any
word in the vocabulary of Christian faith more powerful
than that "Amen – Yes. I believe."

The longer I live, the more convinced I become that the
recitation of the Creed, word after word, statement after
statement, is like our walk through life. We move from day
to week to year, year after year, in what might be compared
to a melodious poetic meter. We hold jobs, sign agreements,

build businesses, get married, make vows, have children, make promises...

But every now and then, something breaks the cadence. A tragedy bolds the font, underlines the memory, italicizes the sorrow. Our very being – body, soul and spirit – sees nothing, hears nothing, beyond the moment when time stands still. Our gut churns at the physician's diagnosis. It writhes to the cacophony of, "I want a divorce." It convulses at the fresh gravesite of a loved one.

I wish life always flowed in harmonious rhyme and meter. But it doesn't. Desperate prayers go unanswered. Heaven sometimes seems so silent our stomachs threaten to heave.

Heartache always leaves a choice in its wake: What do we do with our affirmations and vows when life's rhythm unravels and melody falls into disharmony? What happens to "Amen. Yes, I believe" when our foundations split apart? What shall we do with "the Father Almighty" when He seems oblivious to our tragedy? What shall we say to "He came down from heaven" when hell appears triumphant? Can we say amen to "the giver of life" when death rips a loved one from our arms? Do we believe in "the resurrection of the dead" when despair surrounds us?

Do we say, "Amen. Yes, I *still* believe" to our statements of faith; or do we turn and say nothing?

The prophet Isaiah urged, "Seek the Lord, while He may be found" (Isaiah 55:6). St. James encouraged, "Draw near to God, and He will draw near to you" (James 4:8). Christians with seasoned faith understand there is no shortcut to spiritual maturity, the kind that answers life's agonies with a resounding, "Amen! Yes, I believe." That depth of faith is possible only by God's grace, nurtured as we seek the Lord – day by day – while He may be found; drawing near to Him – day by day – while we have opportunity.

Each time we recite, "Amen" at the end of the Creed, we have a choice. We can say it as part of our religious meter, or

we can say it prayerfully, asking God's grace to enfold us, to help us seek Christ above earthly pleasures, to draw closer to the Savior, to trust Him through variations of life's meter so we might fully trust Him through its cacophony.
Oh God! Help us make it so.

Prayer (from Romans 8): *Father, I know nothing can separate me from Your love. Yet, I ask for Christ's sake, that the confidence in my mind become confidence in my heart. I ask that I – that the Church – shout "Amen" with the apostle Paul's declaration that neither death, nor life, angels, nor principalities, things present, nor things to come, powers, height, depth, nor any other created thing, will separate us from Your love, which is in Christ Jesus my Lord. Amen. And, amen.*

Printed in the United States
86624LV00003B/1-99/A